HELP!
I WORK WITH PEOPLE

HELP!

I WORK WITH PEOPLE

GETTING GOOD AT INFLUENCE, LEADERSHIP, AND PEOPLE SKILLS

CHAD VEACH

BETHANYHOUSE

a division of Baker Publishing Group
Minneapolis, Minnesota

© 2020 by Chad Veach

Published by Bethany House Publishers
11400 Hampshire Avenue South
Bloomington, Minnesota 55438
www.bethanyhouse.com

Bethany House Publishers is a division of
Baker Publishing Group, Grand Rapids, Michigan

Printed in the United States of America

ISBN 978-0-7642-3613-6 (cloth)
ISBN 978-0-7642-3614-3 (paperback)

Unless otherwise indicated, Scripture quotations are taken from the Holy Bible, New Living Translation, copyright © 1996, 2004, 2015 by Tyndale House Foundation. Used by permission of Tyndale House Publishers, Inc., Carol Stream, Illinois 60188. All rights reserved.

Scripture quotations labeled ESV are from The Holy Bible, English Standard Version® (ESV®), copyright © 2001 by Crossway, a publishing ministry of Good News Publishers. Used by permission. All rights reserved. ESV Text Edition: 2016

Scripture quotations labeled NKJV from the New King James Version®. Copyright © 1982 by Thomas Nelson. Used by permission. All rights reserved.

Cover design by Roman Bozhko

Author represented by the Fedd Agency, Inc.

20 21 22 23 24 25 26   7 6 5 4 3

Contents

Contents

Foreword

I am excited for you to hold this book in your hands. I've taught leadership for over forty years now, and I always get excited when new leaders step out with their thoughts on why leadership matters and what it means to lead. I love the variety and creativity they bring to the table to help raise awareness that we are always in search of more leaders who can help transform the world into a better place.

I've known Chad Veach for some time now, and I always come away from my time with him inspired. His commitment to grow in both his character and his skill drives him to become a better person every day, which, in turn, makes him a better leader. But I love the fact that he doesn't stop there—what Chad learns, he also teaches, and his investment in teaching leadership to the coming generations is why I agreed to write this foreword.

Help! I Work with People is a book that every leader should have on their bookshelf. Chad's hunger to pass on what he's learned has resulted a book that communicates more than principles; it captures the heart of leadership, which is *people*. Chad begins where all leadership begins—with yourself—but he quickly shows how to lead with both heart and head, courage and skill.

The book's three sections will help you stay locked in with Chad and his message and provide you with a framework that you'll revisit time and again as you continue on your leadership journey. As we become more aware of the leadership deficit in our world, this book is a needed call for men and women to step forward, take the mantle, and lead with authenticity and passion.

We need leaders like you who will step into this moment and make a difference. *Help! I Work with People* will not only get you started, it will accelerate your growth and prepare you to bring your unique gift of leadership to the world.

Your friend,
John Maxwell

An Invitation to Lead

Leadership has a way of surprising us.

Why? Because leadership is often thrust upon us without warning and without our permission. It might sneak up on us slowly over time, or it might arrive suddenly, almost out of the blue. Regardless of how it happens, there comes a point when we find ourselves coordinating and motivating and managing people, and we usually aren't as ready for it as we would like to be.

Even in those situations where we expected to be hired or promoted to a leadership role, or where we sought a leadership role intentionally, leadership can still surprise us. The actual tasks and day-to-day responsibilities of leadership are hard to predict and can feel surreal. Even after years of experience, we still wonder, at times, what in the world we are doing trying to lead other people.

Because of the surprising nature of leadership, I've often come across people who are doing the work of a leader (and doing it well), but who don't consider themselves leaders. They have influence, they are guiding and directing people, and they are accomplishing goals with their team—but they avoid or reject the title of *leader*. Leadership can seem intimidating, even terrifying. And yet, even if you don't have a job title with the word "leader" or "director" in it, there's a good chance you are already leading in one or more areas. For example:

- Maybe you started your job a few years ago, and over time, you gained enough experience and skill that your boss recently asked you to train and supervise a group of new employees.

9

- Maybe you're a high school teacher, and some of your students have started looking to you for more than just algebra tips: They're asking for your advice about home problems, friend issues, and career choices.
- Maybe you're a parent, and your daughter's soccer team needed a coach, and you somehow found yourself volunteering.
- Maybe you started your own catering business a few years ago and have recently hired a few employees, and now the success of your business depends on whether you can lead other people to do the job far better than you could on your own.
- Maybe you were recently named the youth pastor at your church, and now you have to figure out how to get a bunch of young volunteers to organize and run a weekly youth service.
- Maybe you inherited a family business and the team members you are leading are all older and more experienced than you, but they are looking to you for direction, strategy, and answers.
- Or maybe you were elected president of the school PTA, or you were asked to lead a committee at your church, or you were promoted to department chair.

You get the idea. Leadership happens whether or not you are ready for it and whether or not it comes with a formal title. If you are doing your job well, sooner or later you are likely to be put in charge of other people. Those people have feelings, free will, and ideas of their own, of course, and your challenge is to inspire them to be a unified and productive team. That's when you're likely to say, to quote the title of this book, "Help! I work with people."

Influence, People Skills, and Leadership

Regardless of how you ended up in your current leadership role, there is nothing quite like working with and leading other people. It has its own challenges and rewards, and it requires a unique skill set. When done right, it is beautiful: a group of individuals acting as one, joining forces to accomplish a shared vision. When done wrong, it can be incredibly painful: a group of individuals at odds and in conflict, trying to accomplish something but hurting each other and their goals in the process.

That is why leadership has always fascinated me. Good leaders can make all the difference for the teams they lead. And what makes leaders good is that they know how to influence and work with people, because people are what make up teams. You can't separate leaders from people, and you can't separate leadership from influence.

Leadership is influencing others to work together toward a common goal. Each part of that phrase is important. "Influencing" means that our effectiveness as leaders comes through our ability to motivate others. "Working together" means multiple people each do their part. "Common goal" means the vision is shared by all—the work is a collaboration, not forced labor.

Leadership is influencing others to work together toward a common goal.

Dr. John Maxwell, one of the most recognized names in leadership studies, says, "Leadership is influence—nothing more, nothing less."[1] I fully agree, and throughout this book, I use the terms "leadership" and "influence" interchangeably. You may not have the title of leader, and you may not even think of yourself as a leader, but if you have influence, you are a leader; conversely, a title without influence is nothing more than a sign on the door.

Influence, however, implies *people*. In the definition above, each of the key terms—influence, working together, and common goal—point to the same thing: people. We influence people, we get people to work together, and people have a common goal. Leadership, therefore, is much more relational than many of us realize. So while this is a book about leadership, it is also a book about people: understanding people, serving people, working with people, getting along with people, communicating with people.

Since we can't lead without people, we can't lead well without people skills. I've had the privilege of interviewing numerous well-known leaders in both the church and business world on my podcast, *Leadership Lean In*. Every leader I've interviewed has shared profound principles and wisdom based on their experiences. But what consistently stands out to me is something they rarely mention outright—their people skills. Whether they are naturally gifted or learned along the way, they have figured out that leadership starts and ends with people.

It's worth noting two things here. First, *leaders are also people*. We aren't another species. Our DNA doesn't change just because we have a team, a title, or recognition. As leaders, we will always connect with others most significantly on a human level. That connection is mutual: we give and receive, we teach and learn, we lead and follow, we forgive mistakes and make mistakes. Healthy leaders are people first, then leaders. Remembering that helps us stay grounded.

Second, *people matter*. We don't strive for influence so we can serve ourselves; rather, we strive for influence so we can serve others. Leadership is not about getting people to do what we want. That's why I'm not going to give you ten keys for getting people to fall in line or fifteen principles to stay king of the mountain. Leadership that reduces followers to a nameless mass of people whose purpose is to serve the leader is bad leadership. Every member of a team is first an individual with God-given dreams, needs, and abilities. Leadership is a gift to be valued and stewarded with care because what we do affects people, and people matter.

How to Read This Book

To help you grow your influence, hone your people skills, and improve your leadership, this book is divided into three parts, each of which build on each other.

Part 1 focuses on you as a leader: how to know yourself, lead yourself, and grow yourself. If you hope to influence people, it goes without saying that your influence must be a positive one. That requires a willingness to become self-aware and intentional in all you do and to address your own weaknesses along the way.

Part 2 deals with people skills—everything from manners to reading a room to having a good conversation. This is, in many ways, the heart of the book. If influence is about people, and if you are good at working with people, leadership will often take care of itself. The more you invest in people, the more effective your leadership will be.

Part 3 addresses practical issues related to leading teams, whether that team is part of a business, nonprofit organization, church, or any other organization, large or small. The focus is intentionality—how to accomplish shared goals by applying what you know about yourself and your team in ways that are purposeful, wise, and visionary.

I firmly believe you are called to lead and that your leadership is meant to serve the greater good. Learning to lead well is a never-ending process, but if you approach the challenge with courage and a willingness to grow along the way, great influence—and therefore great good—will be the result.

PART 1

IT'S ALL ABOUT YOU

You are the protagonist in the story that is your life. You can't escape yourself, and you can't operate beyond who and where you are. Who you are as a person will always determine how far you go and how much you accomplish as a leader.

That's not a bad thing. Actually, it should give you hope, because *you* are the only thing you can really control in life. Everything else—circumstances, people, events—is beyond your control. But you have great freedom to shape your own life, which means the choice to become a better friend, parent, teacher, mentor, employer, or leader is up to you. In the chapters that follow, we'll explore topics related to the hardest person you'll ever have to lead: yourself.

ONE

It Starts with You

Leadership always starts with you. Your influence does not begin with the number of people you lead, the size of your budget or salary, the political environment, the stock market, or any other person or circumstance. Your influence begins and ends with who *you* are and with how *you* lead. Those other things have their place, but they don't determine your success. You—not your team or your goals or your mission statement—are the starting point for your leadership and your influence.

I have heard some people say the opposite a few times—that leadership is *not* about the leader, that it has nothing to do with the leader, that the leader should actually be invisible, replaceable, or even anonymous. On the surface, this might sound noble and altruistic because it makes leadership solely about other people, and what could be wrong with that? Just two things: it isn't true, and it doesn't work.

If leadership starts and ends with the people you lead, then you are limited in what you can do if something doesn't seem to be working well or you aren't satisfied with current results. Your only option is to berate, complain, and threaten, hoping your negativity will somehow produce positive results. If you are frustrated with where you are, don't blame everyone else. Study the problem, get counsel, and make needed changes, because leadership starts with you.

Nothing is more counterproductive than blaming the wrong thing when there is a problem. If my car runs out of gas, it's not the weather's fault, or terrible L.A. drivers' fault, or the government's fault. It's my fault. The best course of action is to accept that my wife was right about stopping for gas earlier, to call for help, and then to move on with my day. In the same way, if your leadership is not working, the healthiest and most hope-inducing thing you can do is set your ego or insecurities aside, figure out what is wrong, and fix it. Maybe you are the problem, and maybe you're not. Either way, no one is in a better position than you to identify and fix whatever isn't working—especially if part of the problem is you.

You—with all your quirks and idiosyncrasies, your strengths and weaknesses, your unique journey to get where you are—are the starting point for your own leadership. In accepting that, you discover hope, humility, and the grace to change.

If leadership starts with you, then your first leadership challenge is to lead yourself. You must learn how to teach yourself, guide yourself, and challenge yourself to be the best person and leader you can be. This isn't easy. Admitting that your leadership success depends primarily on you can be uncomfortable at first, because it takes vulnerability and courage to look inward and face the fact that you might need to make some changes. But leading yourself is not only necessary, it is *freeing*. Here are a few reasons why.

1. If You Can Lead Yourself, You Can Lead Anybody

Even if your team includes a difficult person—or a bunch of them—the hardest person you will ever have to lead is yourself. If you can figure out how to lead *you*, you'll be able to lead anyone regardless of their age, experience, or qualifications.

What does it mean to lead yourself? First, *leading yourself means developing self-control*. Self-control is your ability to keep yourself—your emotions, thoughts, goals, and motives—in check and in balance. Are you going to lead from your mind or your emotions? Your will or your whims? Your calling or your comfort? Your spirit or your flesh? When you lead yourself, you become the protagonist rather than the victim of your own story: instead of letting life determine your feelings, thoughts, and reactions, *you* determine them.

Leading yourself means you lead by example. In other words, you practice what you preach. You are authentic, consistent, and honest. You walk beside people rather than pushing them from behind; you take them with you rather than sending them out alone.

To be clear, I'm not saying you have to be a superhero or the expert at everything. That's unrealistic and, honestly, dysfunctional—it's probably not wise for you to try to teach your accountant how to balance the books or tell your graphic designer how to make great art. But when it comes to values, to vision, to integrity, to bravery, to hard work, to humility, and even to following the rules, the best leaders lead by example.

Leading yourself means pursuing personal growth. You have to be strong to lead: mentally strong, morally strong, emotionally strong. It's difficult to lead with authenticity if you are hiding a guilty conscience. It's difficult to stay focused on the future if you're bitter and have a grudge against someone from your past. And it's difficult to stay focused on achieving a goal if you haven't learned to say no to the distractions and sideshows that line the way.

No one is born a perfect leader: it's something you grow into. You have to learn and mature in many areas over time. This kind of growth is normal, and it should be embraced, even celebrated.

Take emotional intelligence, for example, which we'll look at in a later chapter. Learning how to understand and control your emotions is a lifelong process—even if you're not a leader. I have four children, and none of them started out life in control of their feelings. They had to develop control over time, and they still have a long way to go. Not that I blame them—I still have a long way to go as well. It's only to be expected that leaders will need to intentionally focus on developing their emotional intelligence as they grow in influence and authority.

The same is true for every area of personal and leadership growth. Becoming a good leader is a process of gaining knowledge, and learning maturity and skills—and you are the student. Leading yourself is your first and most difficult task, and one that you'll undertake and be challenged by the rest of your life. Don't coast on what you already know. Don't assume weaknesses or deficiencies will take care of themselves as you go along. Take responsibility for who you are, and don't be afraid to face the things you need to learn, change, or fix.

Learning and changing are positives, not negatives. What you learn about yourself—your motivations, your fears, your needs—will inform your leadership and infuse it with authenticity. It will also help you to cultivate essential character traits such as humility, empathy, and relatability. We lead human beings, after all, so it just makes sense that we lead with, lead from, and lead through our own humanity. We lead and influence people with flaws, and so we need to develop the practice of addressing our own flaws.

Ultimately, it is no one else's responsibility to lead you—that responsibility is yours alone. Even if you report to a leader, mentor, boss, or other authority figure, the most that leader can do is guide your external actions; you are responsible for the internal you. And the better you lead yourself, the better you will lead others.

2. If You Can Lead Yourself, Your Weaknesses Won't Stop You

A commitment to self-leadership is a commitment to facing our own limitations—and that can be a hard pill to swallow. Leaders are supposed to have all the answers, right? So, doesn't it undermine our leadership if we admit we might have a problem—or even be the problem? The short answer: *No.* Good leaders can take responsibility for their weaknesses without being undermined or overwhelmed by them.

When I say your "weaknesses" won't stop you, I'm referring to anything that limits your leadership or slows your progress as a team. Most of the time, these are simply the byproducts of being human. Maybe you aren't good at administration, budgets, schedules, or planning. Maybe you don't know how to lead an effective meeting. Maybe you hate answering emails. Maybe you tend to freeze up when facing tough decisions. Maybe you speak so boldly and bluntly that you hurt people. Maybe you can't stand negotiation or conflict. Whatever your limitation is, it's not insurmountable—unless you refuse to acknowledge it.

Why are we so hesitant to confront our own limitations? Often it boils down to insecurity. We're afraid the people we lead will find out what we always suspected to be true: that we aren't enough; that we don't measure up; that we are a fraud and a failure. We convince ourselves it's better to avoid the facts and live in fear than to face reality and risk our self-esteem and our image taking a public hit. So we blame others, blame the economy, blame the government, blame bad luck—and in the process become our own lid, our own ceiling. But we will never grow—personally or as leaders—beyond our capacity to be honest with ourselves and transparent with others when it comes to our limitations.

Once you recognize your limitations, you can overcome them or at least work around them. Sometimes this will mean learning and growing in order to strengthen a weakness. Take a class, read a book, ask questions, get feedback—do whatever you can to improve yourself. Other times, rather than fixing a weakness, you will need to staff your weakness. If you can't keep up with your email inbox, consider giving someone on your administrative team that job. If you can't negotiate well but you have to broker a deal, take someone along who handles conflict better than you. There is no shame in admitting you'll never be great in

Your authority comes less from your ability and more from your authenticity.

a particular area and delegating the task to someone else. In my experience, my team already knows where I'm weak, and it bothers them a lot less than I would have thought. Far from being condemning or feeling disappointed in my leadership, they are eager to help by filling in my weaknesses with their strengths.

I'm not saying leadership abilities aren't important—people tend to stop following inept leaders sooner rather than later. But I am saying your willingness to be honest, humble, and courageous in facing your weaknesses is far more important. You can staff or organize your way around a lack of skills, but first you have to acknowledge what you lack.

3. If You Can Lead Yourself, You Will Inspire People to Follow

The story is told that when John Wesley, the famous eighteenth-century preacher, was asked how he attracted such large crowds, he replied, "I set myself on fire and people come to watch me burn."[1] In other words, people are watching you, and they will be attracted by your passion, drive, and commitment.

Leaders who lead themselves are leaders who are internally motivated: they have identified, developed, and refined the "why" behind what they are doing. They are self-motivated, therefore they can motivate others; they are self-inspired, therefore they can inspire others. They are passionate about the vision that drives them, and their passion is a magnet that draws people to their cause.

It's worth mentioning that not all motives are good motives. Part of leading yourself is making sure you are in control of the hidden drivers behind your actions, decisions, and words. Why? Because sooner or later, the motives of your heart will be revealed, and they will affect your long-term leadership success. If things like fear, greed, power, lust, and anger are lurking behind your leadership, you'll have a tough time keeping a solid team, because no one wants to follow that kind of leader for long. However, if you are motivated by things like love, faith, compassion, a dream of a better world, the potential of your team, and building others up, you will inspire long-term loyalty and passion in your followers. Your ability to own and lead your own heart will stir the hearts of those who follow you.

ooo

Your leadership starts with you, which means you can begin leading *right now* by deciding to lead yourself. Will you assume responsibility for who you are and the influence you have? Will you be honest with your strengths and weaknesses? Will you keep your motives pure and your passion strong? Will you commit to the process of authenticity, growth, learning, and change? When you accept that you and you alone are the most important factor in your own leadership, you set yourself

22

up for even greater levels of influence and leadership. Your journey begins with you.

KEY TAKEAWAY

Your influence with others begins with who you are and how well you lead yourself.

TWO

The Most Important Investment

LeBron James will undoubtedly be remembered as one of the greatest players in basketball history. His stats are consistently jaw-dropping, despite competing in a sport that is usually dominated by younger players. His manager, Mav Carter, revealed in an interview with NBA reporter Alex Kennedy one of the reasons for LeBron's consistent performance: he spends about $1.5 million a year on his body. Let that number sink in for a second: *$1.5 million every year.* That includes things like cryotherapy, hyperbaric chambers, exotic leg boots, exercise routines, diet, and much more. In Kennedy's words: "He invested in his body, so he can still dominate at 33 years old."[1]

Top athletes typically don't divulge how much money they spend on their bodies and their health, but LeBron's expenses may not be as outlandish as they sound. For example, Russell Wilson, elite quarterback for the Seattle Seahawks, has a performance team dedicated to his well-being, including a movement specialist, a massage therapist, a mental coach, a trainer, and a chef. "Putting the team in place is like having a Formula One car," he says. "You have to make sure that everything's tuned up and ready to roll. I want my car to be driving like Lewis Hamilton, and flying around those corners."[2]

The most important number, though, isn't the amount these athletes spend on caring for their bodies, but the return they get on their investments.

LeBron's career earnings were recently estimated at over *$1 billion*.[3] With that kind of return, spending a million or two a year isn't exorbitant: it's an investment that pays incredible dividends.

A common myth of leadership is that great leaders are naturally great. They don't have to work at it like the rest of us do, the myth says—they just coast along on their innate greatness. But that would be like saying LeBron James and Russell Wilson coast on their athletic ability, and nothing could be further from the truth: they work relentlessly and passionately on every aspect of their game. Sure, they have natural gifts and abilities, but they have also multiplied those gifts and abilities many times over through training and hard work. They invest in themselves, and their investment pays off.

The same could be said for every sport, skill, or profession in the world, including leadership. Some people are naturally gifted, but no one is naturally great. Everyone has to work at what they do. Everyone has to invest in themselves: in their craft, in their art, in their game.

Do the Work

No matter how much raw leadership talent you were born with, your long-term effectiveness will depend on what you do with the talent you have now. Will you develop it, strengthen it, and share it? Or will you coast along, hoping that lackluster effort will somehow produce great influence?

Scientific research backs up the idea that investment in leadership ability matters. This is a key point, because for decades (or maybe centuries), leadership theorists have argued over whether leaders are born or made. Are leadership traits predetermined or can they be learned? How does a leader emerge? Is leadership the result of nature or nurture?

If leaders are *born*, then not everyone can be a leader, or at least not a great leader. According to this perspective, if you aren't naturally gifted, or if you've never held a leadership role, or if you don't come from a family of leaders, then maybe you aren't "meant" to lead. This approach places a high value on inborn traits, such as your personality and gifts, and essentially states that only certain kinds of people make effective leaders.

On the other hand, if leaders are *made*, then innate gifts play no role and you could theoretically become as great a leader as the amount of effort you're willing to put into it. According to this perspective, anyone can be a great leader if they just work hard enough.

It's an argument that may never be fully resolved, but scientific research has shown what most of us probably already suspected: there is some truth to both perspectives. One study focused on factors that influenced what it called "leadership role occupancy," which simply means "holding a leadership position." The study analyzed 238 sets of identical twins (who share 100 percent of their genetic background) and compared them to 188 sets of fraternal twins (who share only 50 percent of their genetic background). The analysis revealed that 30 percent of an individual's leadership role occupancy could be attributed to genetic factors, and the remainder to non-shared environmental factors.[4] In other words, nearly one-third of their leadership role could be related to traits they were born with, while over two-thirds was not. In another study, researchers also found support for the "born leader" idea, and they even went so far as to identify a specific genotype, rs4950, that was associated with leadership role occupancy. In this study, researchers found the genetic portion of leadership role occupancy to be 24 percent. They concluded that leadership role occupancy is "the complex product of genetic and environmental influences."[5]

These studies indicate that, indeed, there is a degree to which some people naturally tend toward leadership. But before you write yourself off by saying "I'm not a born leader," note the percentages these studies revealed: only 24 to 30 percent of leadership role occupancy is related to genetics. That means anywhere from 70 to 76 percent depends on factors you can (at least to some extent) control, such as environment, training, hard work, opportunities, and persistence. Leaders are both born *and* made, but mostly made. Even if your genes are not in your favor, so to speak, your DNA doesn't determine your leadership destiny—not even close.

Your leadership potential depends on you, not your family tree.

The research is fascinating, but honestly, you don't have to be a scientist to realize that leaders are mostly made. Simple observation of great leaders bears this out: you would be hard-pressed to find a specific style, personality, or background that is better than others when it comes to leadership. Great leaders may share some qualities, skills, and values, but neither science nor human experience support the idea that *only* born leaders can be successful in leadership, or that born leaders will *automatically* be successful at leadership.

Therefore, you can *choose* to become a leader. Even more important, you can choose to become a great leader, an effective leader, an influential leader. You make that choice by investing in yourself and your leadership role. You can't control everything in your environment, but you can control a lot. And if you're willing to invest in your leadership development, you can take whatever gifts, abilities, knowledge, and resources you start with and multiply them many times over.

Four Essential Investments

Investing in yourself and your leadership development is not selfish—it's wise. You might not be worth a billion dollars this year, but you are worth a lot to your team and others around you. You owe it to them to take care of yourself and become the best possible version of yourself. As the leader goes, so goes the team. You can't lead from an unhealthy place and expect those you lead to be healthy. Whether you are healthy or unhealthy, your mental, physical, and spiritual condition will affect team culture and dynamics. If you're healthy, your leadership can have a positive impact on those you lead. And if you're unhealthy, your leadership can negatively affect individuals who consider you a role model and pattern their lives after yours. You can't give more than you receive. As soon as you start deficit spending, it's only a matter of time until you're done.

Investments are, by definition, proactive—you make an investment before you need it, not after. When it comes to personal and leadership development, investing in yourself means taking action now to stay healthy and strong—in the present and for the future. LeBron James and Russell Wilson didn't wait until they were injured to start taking care of themselves, and neither should you.

To help you get started, here are four essential investments you can make to stay healthy and strong for the long haul.

1. Invest in Community

Don't lead alone and don't live your life alone. No matter how introverted you are, you need people. No matter how successful you are, you still depend on people. People keep you grounded and sane. They remind you why you do what you do. They give you input and feedback that is usually unsolicited but actually helps a lot. They rein you in when you move too fast, encourage you when you move too slow, call you out when you start to get a little weird, and help you to be the best possible version of yourself.

A while back, my wife, Julia, asked me what I would like to do for my upcoming birthday, maybe a big party, a family trip, or dinner out. Life had been very busy, and I found myself longing to simply be among friends. "I really just want to have a few close friends over to hang out," I told her. So that's what we did, and it was incredibly rejuvenating: no pressure, no agenda, no expectations. Nothing but community.

Don't let leadership isolate you. That is one of the worst things you can do. Surround yourself with friends who will love you and accept you through difficult times. Find people who are willing to tell you what you need to hear, with love and boldness. Build a team of people who are strong in the areas where you are weak. Stay connected with people who need you and draw from you, because the essence of leading is giving, and if you become isolated, you lose access to the very heart of leadership.

2. Invest in Time Off

Build "unproductivity" into your schedule. You need blocks of time on your calendar in which you are not producing anything. Time off. Rest days. Vacation. For highly driven people, that can be frustrating, but highly driven people are typically the ones who need to do this the most. Even your body knows you can't work all the time. Have you ever wondered why you have to sleep every night? Maybe it's a gentle reminder that you're not God. You're a human being, and you need to rest.

Investing in time off could mean spending the day with your family, taking a vacation, enjoying a hobby, playing sports, reading a book, catching up on SportsCenter news, binge-watching Netflix with your significant other, or doing just about anything that is not inherently work. You need romantic time with your spouse and quality time with your kids. You need time to explore new interests, to be creative, to be spontaneous, to be lazy, to be slow.

I'm not going to tell you to work only eight hours a day, or to take one day off a week, or to go on vacation three weeks out of the year. Those decisions are up to you. But if you're not intentional about it—if you don't value it enough to put it on your calendar and protect it—you're setting yourself up for a greater loss later. It's better to sacrifice some short-term productivity now than it is to blow out an adrenal gland later and have to take a year off, and maybe never be the same again.

3. Invest in Professional Development

Prioritize your professional development by making it part of your job responsibilities. Read books, attend conferences and retreats, join professional networks and associations, have conversations with peers and mentors—do whatever you can to keep learning. The moment you choose to stop learning is the moment you choose to fail, because it will only be a matter of time before you fall behind the times or others pass you by. You will never arrive, so make a commitment now never to stop learning.

For the last two decades, I've made it my goal to learn everything I can about leadership. It's a fascinating topic to me, and I've read countless books written by people I've never met but who I consider heroes and mentors. More recently, I've had the privilege of interviewing a number of well-known leaders for my podcast, *Leadership Lean In*, and those conversations have expanded my views in ways I couldn't have foreseen. As leaders, it is vital to get outside of our bubble—our culture, our experiences, our relationships—and to intentionally invite others to speak into our lives.

4. Invest in Building a Trusted Team

There's a scene in the Pixar movie *Cars* in which the main character, Lightning McQueen, a stock car, refuses to allow his pit crew to do their jobs because he wants to get back on the track and keep his lead. Predictably, he burns out his tires and loses the race. As a leader, you need to let your team do their jobs. You need them, and they need you. No one wins when a leader tries to do everything solo.

Trusting your team starts before the race, though. Trust is built over time by working together, training together, and talking together. Build a team you can trust, and then trust your team. If someone fails, don't retract your trust. Just train them better, then trust again. As trust grows, you'll find your team will become an extension of you—but it will be a better version of you than you could ever be on your own.

If you feel chronically exhausted and frustrated, it could be an indication that either you're not trusting the people you have with enough of the load, or that you need more people to share the load. Instead of cutting back or burning out, try looking for new team members to fill the gaps. Put out a call for volunteers or offer job training and see who is interested. Maybe take another look at your current team members and see who might be able to take on a new or expanded role. Respond to pressure by building a better team, not by taking everything into your own hands.

ooo

Investing in yourself is not a onetime decision or a short-term practice. To maximize the return on your investment, you have to think long term—about where you want to be in five years, ten years, thirty years. Then make decisions and investments now that will get you where you want to be over time. A good friend of mine, *New York Times* bestselling author and speaker Judah Smith, often talks about his goal of being "better at seventy," and that's a great way to keep life in perspective. Decades from now, what will matter most? That you closed one more deal, made one more sale, started one more church, traveled to one more country, won one more championship, developed one more product? Those things are not insignificant, but your family, friends, and team would probably agree that *you* are more important than your achievements.

Unless you're LeBron James, you can probably skip the hyperbaric chambers and exotic leg boots, but don't skip investing in yourself. Your team and your family need you whole for a long time to come.

KEY TAKEAWAY

An investment in yourself as a leader is an investment in your team and your future together.

THREE

Find Your Strengths

My staff and I recently took a personality test. I love personality tests for two reasons: first, because they help me know myself better; and second, because I like reading the lists of strengths associated with my personality type. It's a total confidence booster. I've never struggled too much with self-esteem, to be honest. After taking this particular test, a few of us were texting back and forth about our results in a group text and discovered that two of us had the same personality type.

"Isn't this list of strengths amazing?" I posted. "I love this! Nailed it."

Just after I sent my message, my personality twin sent one of her own: "That list of weaknesses! Wow . . . describes me so well!"

"What?" I replied. "There was a list of negatives?"

To be honest, I hadn't even noticed that there were negatives because I was too busy looking at the positives. We shared a good laugh over it, mostly at my expense, but I don't think it's necessarily a bad thing to be more aware of your strengths than your weaknesses. For me, at least, it's a lot more motivating.

Self-awareness is about knowing your strengths and weaknesses, but leadership is primarily about influencing from your strengths. You can't move forward if you are forever self-analyzing. Identify the skills or strengths you lack and either grow in those areas or staff them. But don't stand there, gazing longingly through the window at the leadership gifts you wish you could have. You have your own gifts, and the sooner you discover them and put them to use, the easier and more effective your leadership will be.

Donald O. Clifton was an influential psychologist, educator, author, and researcher, particularly in the area of strength-based psychology. He dedicated much of his career to helping companies improve their businesses by focusing on their employees' strengths. In *Now, Discover Your Strengths,* Clifton and coauthor Marcus Buckingham state this:

> Our research into human strengths does not support the extreme, and extremely misleading, assertion that "you can play any role you set your mind to," but it does lead us to this truth: Whatever you set your mind to, *you will be most successful when you craft your role to play to your signature talents* [strengths] *most of the time.*[1]

In other words, figure out what you are hardwired to be the best at, and work as hard as you can at that. You actually *can't* be anybody you want to be, and you definitely can't be everybody. You can only be yourself, which means the most effective use of your time is to pursue what you have the potential to be great at. Clifton and Buckingham go on to say:

> To avoid your strengths and to focus on your weaknesses isn't a sign of diligent humility. It is almost irresponsible. By contrast the most responsible, the most challenging, and, in the sense of being true to yourself, the most honorable thing to do is face up to the strength potential inherent in your talents and then find ways to realize it.[2]

There is no one personality, background, or mix of gifts that is perfectly and exclusively suited for leadership. But the traits *least* suited to your leadership are the ones you don't have. Sometimes people hide behind what they think they are missing because it's easier than using what they have. For example, they refuse to lead a committee because they aren't good at speaking in front of groups, or they reject a new career opportunity because they don't think they are smart enough to learn something new. But you can work with the traits you have. Are you an introvert? Then you're in good company with creative innovators such as Albert Einstein, Bill Gates, and J.K. Rowling. Were you a poor student? So were

John D. Rockefeller, Thomas Edison, and Walt Disney. Did you have a difficult childhood? So did Oprah, Charlize Theron, and Jim Carrey. Have you failed or been rejected multiple times? Same with Steven Spielberg, Stephen King, and Jay-Z.

I'm not minimizing your challenges, because those things are very real, but I am saying that whatever those things are, they aren't the whole story about you. You are empowered for leadership not by what you don't have, but by what you do have. The only traits, skills, and advantages you can use are the ones you possess and develop, so don't waste time wishing for all the other ones.

Identify Your Gifts

In order to use your leadership gifts, you have to identify them. Personality tests are a great tool, but they are just a start. And it's worth keeping in mind that some of your gifts and strengths might not appear until many years down the road, which means you need to be continually assessing your gifts and how best to use them. Here are five questions you can ask yourself—and others—to help you pinpoint your gifts.

1. What Comes Naturally to Me?

When you look back to your childhood and young adulthood, what traits, interests, or abilities stand out to you? Were you always able to make people laugh? Constantly tinkering with technology? Fascinated by numbers and science? Captivated by beauty in art and nature? Did social skills or emotional intelligence seem easy for you? What creative skills did you learn quickly? How did you stand out from the crowd among your peers? All of those things could help you in leadership if you lean into them rather than longing for something you don't have. Comparison is often a trap, but when used to identify your gifts, it can also help you to recognize where you have the potential to truly excel.

For example, I'm pretty good at talking. I have been since I was child, although I didn't always see that as a positive (and my parents probably didn't either). I'm not saying it's easy to stand in front of a crowd or meet new people—sometimes it can be quite difficult—but it's something I am able to do well and I enjoy. It's not a coincidence that a large part of my job has to do with talking, whether in public or in smaller settings. Over the years, not only have I embraced opportunities to speak in public, but I've also worked on improving my speaking gifts. I'm also relatively good at basketball, but that one didn't really take me anywhere. So, I mostly stick with talking.

Maybe you're the opposite: you speak in public only when you have no other choice. Maybe you prefer to be in the background, to speak last in meetings, and to put other people on the stage, but you find yourself in a leadership position. The fact that you don't thrive on public speaking doesn't make you less of a leader—as long as you are using the gifts you do have to their greatest advantage.

2. What Do Other People Observe in Me?

It's been said that fish don't know there's water. It's so much a part of their reality that they can't see it. A similar dynamic can happen with our gifts and skills—they're so much a part of us that we can't see them.

If you are naturally good at something, or if you've honed your skills in some area because you enjoyed it, you might not realize how talented you are. It feels natural and easy for you, and so you assume it feels natural and easy for everyone—that is, until other people point out that whatever it is *doesn't* come easily for them. This is something unique to you.

What have other people observed in you over the years? What were you recognized for when you were a kid, a teenager, or a young adult? What natural traits or skills do people tend to observe in you now? If you don't know, take the initiative and ask a few people to tell you what they've observed in you.

When trusted people in your life notice and affirm your gifts, listen to them. Resist the temptation to downplay your gifts. Denying what you're good at isn't humility, it's just denial. True humility is recognizing who you are—nothing more, nothing less—with gratitude and grace.

3. What Have I Learned by Trial and Error?

This is also known as failure, but "trial and error" sounds better. Trial and error is the process of trying things, failing, learning from failure, and trying again. And again. And maybe again. Learning by failure is an inevitable part of the human existence, but that doesn't make it any less painful. No one likes to fail, but sometimes it's the only consistent path to improvement. You might be lucky enough to get things right the first time in a couple of areas, but to err is human, so you should probably get used to it.

When it comes to determining your gifts, trial and error plays a key role. Why? Because you don't start out knowing what you are good at. You have to try a lot of things a lot of times, which means failing a lot of times too. If you truly believe something might be part of your future, don't give up just because you fail or aren't good at it right away. On the other hand, it's also important to stay open to the possibilities—it's surprising how often life tricks us into doing things we would have never imagined ourselves doing, yet we turn out to be good at them and enjoy them.

Learning through trial and error is less about the error and more about the learning. In other words, you're going to fail a lot. But where do you learn the most? Where do you grow, change, and try again, even if no one around you seems to care? More likely than not, you are gifted in that area, and it's up to you to develop it further. For example, I can tell you the subtle difference between various cuts of shirts or kinds of shoes because I care about fashion; when it comes to auto mechanics, I can't tell a transmission from an axle. I have learned through trial and error that I love fashion but couldn't care less about cars.

4. What Do I Enjoy?

The best leaders have an innate desire to do what they're doing. Many say they'd do it even if they weren't paid for it, or they get so wrapped up in it that hours fly by and they hardly realize the passage of time. So, what is that for you? What do you have a desire to do? What would you do even if you weren't paid for it? What makes time fly?

Even when you're focused on doing what you enjoy, you might feel discouraged once in a while, but if it's truly your calling, you should feel disappointed at the thought of giving it up. Something deep inside you will be drawn toward the challenge and the potential, and you'll push through any resistance to accomplish it. Conversely, if you feel relieved at the prospect of not doing something, it's likely time to move on or to delegate whatever it is. Enjoyment is often an indicator of talent.

5. What Works for Me?

If you have clear success in an area, if you feel the wind at your back, if you sense God smiling on you, chances are good you're doing something right. Maybe you've heard the term "in your wheelhouse" to refer to something that is within your area of expertise. The term "wheelhouse" comes from the nautical world and refers to the location of a ship's wheel. But it has also been used more recently in baseball to describe a batter's strike zone—the area in which the player swings with the most force and effectiveness.[3] When we say a task is in our wheelhouse, it means we're good at it. It's an area where we operate with force and effectiveness.

Some things are just in your wheelhouse. You might not be able to explain it, you might not have chosen it, you might even get tired of it, but you just know how to do certain things. And when you do them, they work, and you and everyone around you knows it.

I mentioned that I have always been a talker, but that doesn't mean I always knew my calling was public speaking. I remember when I realized that, though, and it was because someone else pointed out my effectiveness and results. At the time, I had already been speaking in public for seven or eight years, mostly at youth events. One day, an older pastor in my city invited me to lunch. I was nervous, to be honest; I halfway assumed I had done something wrong. So I was surprised when he asked, "How did you become such a good speaker?"

I assured him I was not a good speaker, and I meant what I said. I knew how to throw a good afterparty, I told him. Although I spent a lot of time studying for my talks, I had never considered myself to be a particularly talented speaker.

"Yes," he said, "you are a good speaker. I know you are, because my son comes home Sunday night after listening to you and repeats every word you said."

At that moment, a light bulb came on in my head. I *was* good at this—not because I necessarily felt good at it, but because I was effective at it. And that realization made me want to work harder to get even better.

Everyone Is a Genius

When it comes to leadership gifts, I like to use the word "genius." Genius isn't some supernatural, magical, miraculous ability—it's just an *uncommon* ability, a unique quality or aptitude for something. Someone who is a genius in a particular area is remarkably gifted in comparison to the average person. Albert Einstein was a physics genius. Bach was a musical genius. Kobe Bryant was a basketball genius.

The reason I like this word is because everyone is a genius if you just get to know them. Everyone has genius in their own way and in their own areas, and successful leadership requires tapping in to that genius—both your own and others'. You can call it gifting, skill, expertise, or calling, but at the end of the day, it's simply a skill or quality that makes you remarkable.

"As soon as you find yourself in a role that requires you to play to one of your nontalents—or area of low skills or knowledge—a weakness is born."

—Buckingham and Clifton

You might have genius in multiple areas, or perhaps in just one. Maybe your genius is social media, or graphic design, or communication, or hosting events, or reading people. Maybe your genius is surrounding yourself with other geniuses—motivating and caring for them and uniting them into a team. If you don't know what your genius is, follow the steps above to find out. Then spend most of your time and energy on that.

This truth is not to be taken lightly. We can actually cause significant damage by attempting to operate outside of our genius or the areas in which we are gifted. Buckingham and Clifton explore this idea in-depth.[4]

That's sobering.

Instead of wishing you were someone you are not or trying to be someone you will never be, learn what your genius is, lean in to it, and love who you are.

ooo

Learn to appreciate your strengths, your gifts, and your genius, and learn to appreciate those of others as well. That might mean taking a personality test, like I did with my team. It might mean working together for a while and seeing who fits where. And it might mean long and sometimes painful conversations about how to work together. Ultimately, the goal is not about who is *bad* at what (that is, the weakness list), but rather it is about who is *good* at what (the strength list). If you figure that out, and if you learn to work together and play to your strengths, you'll be unstoppable.

KEY TAKEAWAY

Learn to identify, develop, and build on your strengths, and help your team do the same.

FOUR

Love Yourself, Lead Yourself

Everyone has issues. No debate there. When it comes to leading fallible people, most leaders know that they have to show mercy and grace, give people space, believe the best about others, and focus on potential as well as problems. But how do we as leaders treat our own fallible selves? Do we show ourselves the same grace we extend to others? This is important because we can't lead ourselves unless we love ourselves.

If you're anything like me, love and grace are probably not your first reactions when you come face-to-face with your failures or weaknesses. My first response is often shame. I feel embarrassed. I hope no one notices or gets hurt. On the one hand, it's normal to feel embarrassed, but I also know that embarrassment can quickly escalate to shame, and shame is a bully—especially for leaders, who can bully themselves incessantly.

Researcher and bestselling author Brené Brown has spent years studying the effects of shame on people's lives and, conversely, the importance of vulnerability. Her TEDx talk, "The Power of Vulnerability," has amassed over forty-five million views and is one of the top TED talks of all time.

Dr. Brown's message is that you can't be vulnerable without knowing how to handle shame. You will face criticism and failure, so you will feel shame from time to time. But you don't have to live in shame, and you don't have to be shut down by shame. Instead, you can embrace vulnerability. How? By separating your worth as a person from your function as a leader.

When you get to a place where you understand that love and belonging, your worthiness, is a birthright and not something you have to earn, anything is possible. Keep worthiness off the table. Your raise can be on the table, your promotion can be on the table, your title can be on the table, your grades can be on the table. But keep your worthiness for love and belonging off the table. And then ironically everything else just takes care of itself.[1]

You are worthy of love, not because of what you accomplish, but simply because you are a human being. You are innately and immeasurably valuable, and nothing—not even failure—can take that away. Ironically, Dr. Brown herself received a great deal of criticism after her TEDx talk went viral. She acknowledges that the experience was difficult, but that it has also made her more convinced than ever of the truth of what she teaches. The key is to develop what she often refers to as "shame resilience," which is the ability to process shame in a healthy way by separating worth from performance.

> When you lose your capacity to care what other people think, you've lost your ability to connect. But when you're defined by it, you've lost your ability to be vulnerable. That tightrope is what my talk is about, and I think that balance bar we carry is shame resilience. I think it's the thing that keeps us steady. If we can understand that: I'm not the best comment, I'm not the best accolade I've received, and I'm not the worst. This is my work.[2]

If you don't learn to value and love yourself—to separate your worth from the things you accomplish, the praise you receive, or the goals you reach—you won't lead yourself. Why? Because you won't believe in yourself enough to really try. And if you don't love yourself, you won't follow yourself, either, because why would you want to follow a leader who despises you, even if that leader is you? Hating yourself and shaming yourself is doubly unmotivating. You'll stop listening to that God-given voice within that believes in you, encourages you to try, and gives you pep talks to keep going. You'll become your own biggest critic and your own most vicious hater.

It's been said that you teach others how to treat you by how you treat yourself. If you don't respect yourself, others won't either. If you don't think

41

what you have to say is important, others won't listen. That's why you can't allow others to tell you how to feel about yourself. The way people treat you is shaped, to a great extent, by the way you treat yourself.

It's important to get this right, because ultimately, you'll treat others the way you treat yourself. Brené Brown says, "You can't raise children who have more shame resilience than you do. Because even if you don't shame them, and even if you are actively trying to raise them feeling good about who they are, they're never going to treat themselves better than you treat yourself."[3] That's a truth that applies to more than just your children: it applies to everyone you lead.

In the church community my wife and I pastor, there is a man who made a series of poor choices that wreaked havoc on his marriage and family. Over a period of months, things went from bad to worse. Finally, at the end of himself, he decided to make a change. He wanted to put his life back together as much as possible, and he sought counsel from leaders at our church.

At that point, I had to decide how to react. There was plenty of opportunity for shame because the man's mistakes were obvious to all. I could have responded, "What were you thinking? You should have known this would happen." Instead, I chose patience, grace, and acceptance. He already knew he had blown it and made a mess of things. Now he needed help, encouragement, and most of all, unconditional love. He needed acceptance, not shame. Acceptance does not condone mistakes, but it helps people recover from mistakes. It helps them forgive, heal, and hope again.

To lead others in a non-shaming way—to create an environment that promotes security and vulnerability—you have to give yourself room to fail. You can't be cruel to yourself. You can't be intolerant of yourself. I often find that the mean people are first and foremost meanest to themselves. They're upset about their failures, their decisions, their actions. They loathe themselves and take it out on others. You don't want to be that kind of leader.

On a deep level, you need to be convinced that you are good, beautiful, and valuable. Period. Your work is an extension of you, but it doesn't define you. It reflects you and is part of your contribution to the world, but your success or failure at work doesn't add to or subtract from your worth. You will never be more worthy than you are today.

Along with "shame resilience," I'd like to suggest we add "fame resilience" to our arsenal. Fame, which includes any form of widespread recognition and praise, can be just as damaging as shame.

That is the only way to stand strong against the condemnation and criticism, the flattery and celebrity, that come with leadership. Leading is not easy. But without a solid sense of identity and self-worth, it's virtually impossible.

Just to clarify, loving yourself is not the same as idealizing yourself or making yourself the center of the universe. The word for that kind of behavior is *narcissism*—and narcissism and leadership don't play well together. There is a difference between self-worship and self-love.

When you love yourself, you value yourself. It's not vanity or selfishness; it's simply acknowledging the truth: you are of infinite worth, and so is every other human on the planet. To love yourself doesn't mean loving yourself to the exclusion of everyone else.

> *Both shame and fame lose their power to corrupt us when they are detached from our worth.*

Nor does it mean loving yourself *more* than everyone else, or even loving yourself *as much as* everyone else. Comparisons such as these do everyone a disservice because your value is completely independent of those around you, and their value is also independent of you.

The objective is this: *Love yourself so you can love everybody else.* Not only should we love others, but it is both good and necessary to love ourselves along the way. We won't love others very effectively if we despise ourselves.

It's also worth noting that love and approval are not the same thing. I love my children, but I don't approve of everything they do—not by a long shot. Loving yourself doesn't mean you are proud of everything you've done or even who you are at this point in time. You probably have some character issues or patterns of behavior that need to be addressed, and you probably already know what they are. Shame, guilt, and self-loathing are not going to get you where you want to go, but vulnerability

43

might, especially when it's combined with humility, self-acceptance, self-confidence, grace, and mercy.

ooo

As leaders, we can make a point of shaming less. We can be intentional about creating environments in which vulnerability can thrive. And we can start with ourselves.

KEY TAKEAWAY

Your ability to love and lead others grows from your ability to love and lead yourself.

FIVE

I Think I Can

Bobby Jones, an influential attorney and golfer who helped found the Augusta Golf Club and the Masters Tournament, once said, "Competitive sports are played mainly on a five-and-a-half-inch court: the space between your ears."[1] He was referring, of course, to the self-talk that is so crucial to an athlete's success—or failure. Sports psychology has long taught that whatever athletes tell themselves, especially under pressure, has a tremendous effect on their performance.

In his autobiography, *Open*, tennis legend Andre Agassi describes the mental focus and self-talk the game requires, both on and off the court.

> Tennis is the sport in which you talk to yourself. No athletes talk to themselves like tennis players. . . . In tennis you're on an island. Of all the games men and women play, tennis is the closest to solitary confinement, which inevitably leads to self-talk, and for me the self-talk starts here in the afternoon shower. This is when I begin to say things to myself, crazy things, over and over, until I believe them.[2]

Anyone who has played amateur sports knows the importance of keeping a positive attitude, of visualizing success. The same goes for other areas of life, including leadership. Some of the most important conversations you will ever have are the ones inside your head. What you tell yourself matters more than you probably realize.

The Power of Self-Talk

We can't always control the random thoughts that come our way, but we can control our self-talk, which refers to the things we say to ourselves about who we are and what we are capable of accomplishing. Controlling these thoughts is an essential skill practiced by leaders who know how to lead themselves, and it's a skill every leader can intentionally develop.

My father-in-law, Bob MacGregor, grew up in a highly dysfunctional home, but he went on to become a respected leader who travels and speaks internationally, training thousands of leaders around the world. At the beginning of his career, when he was surrounded by people who seemed more qualified, more confident, and more "normal," he was bombarded by voices in his head telling him he wasn't enough. He recalls making a conscious decision not to define himself by his past, by his upbringing, by his insecurity, or by his shame. He learned to control his thoughts and emotions by mentally repeating life-giving statements: *Everyone wants me here. I have something to say. My voice matters.* He self-talked his way from anonymity to influence.

Brené Brown, whom I quoted in the last chapter, gives us this advice: "Talk to yourself like you would to someone you love."[3] The way some leaders self-talk not only fails Brené's love standard, it would be considered outright offensive, cruel, or defamatory if the same words were spoken to anyone else. Why do we think it's acceptable or even productive to talk to ourselves with so much negativity? Shame is an accuser, not a leader; and when we shame ourselves in a misguided attempt to motivate ourselves, we actually do the opposite: we become more defensive, fearful, and inhibited.

You will become what you think about most.

You have influence. You have something to say, something to give, something to contribute. Your *I ams* need to be louder than your *I am nots. I am* wanted. *I am* valuable. *I am* here for a reason.

In the case of my father-in-law, he had to beat back lies from his past in order to speak such truths to himself. I was fortunate enough to grow up in a home that instilled life-giving truths in me. I am forever grateful that my mother spoke words of affirmation to me throughout my youth. She said

46

things like, "Everyone wants to hear what you have to say. Every room you walk into is better because you are there." It gave me such confidence, such an advantage in leadership, and it shaped my self-perception in positive ways.

Dr. Shad Helmstetter, author of the bestselling book *What to Say When You Talk to Your Self*, has done extensive research on the role of the brain in human behavior. He writes:

> After you examine the philosophies, the theories, and the practiced methods of influencing human behavior, you'll find, as I did, that it gets down to the truth of one powerful fact: You will become what you think about most; *your success or failure in anything, large or small, will depend on your programming—what you accept from others, and what you say when you talk to yourself. . . . The brain simply believes what you tell it most.* And what you tell it *about you*, it *will* create. It has no choice.[4]

Your thoughts can be your ally or your enemy. You can choose to leverage the brain's incredible creative potential to support your goals or to hinder them. It comes down to what you choose to think about most.

The Importance of Self-Efficacy

"Self-efficacy" is a term that describes a person's opinion and judgment of "how well one can execute courses of action required to deal with prospective situations."[5] In other words, it's not a measure of how well people actually perform, but of how *confident they are* that they will be able to perform well. The term was first proposed by psychologist Albert Bandura, whose extensive research documents the direct and wide-ranging connection between what we *think* we can do and what we actually *do.*

Bandura states that people tend to "avoid activities that they believe exceed their coping capabilities, but they undertake and perform assuredly those that they judge themselves capable of managing."[6] That connection makes sense: why attempt something if you're certain you'll fail? Self-doubt will cut short your leadership impact before it even starts. On the other hand, if you are confident in your abilities, you will step boldly into leadership positions.

As a parent, I try to build my son's confidence whenever I can. Every day when I drop him off at preschool, I tell him three things I love about him, and they are nearly always identity things: "I love how confident you are. I love that you are kind to people. I love your sense of humor." He always gets a cute little smirk on his face when I begin, but I can tell he loves it. Sometimes we'll even talk for a few seconds about what those phrases mean and what they look like practically. I know that if he shows up to class confident, it will affect his entire day: how he does in class, how he relates to his friends, how he tackles new areas of learning, how he handles his mistakes, and how he stands up to potential bullying or criticism.

How you face challenges depends on how you see yourself. Bandura states, "When beset with difficulties, people who entertain serious doubts about their capabilities slacken their efforts or give up altogether, whereas those who have a strong sense of efficacy exert greater effort to master the challenges."[7]

In other words, difficulties are less likely to stop you if you believe in yourself. Why? Because if you doubt yourself, you'll give up at the first hint of failure; but if you truly believe in yourself, you'll redouble your efforts in the face of failure. Often the biggest obstacle is not the obstacle itself, but rather your view of yourself.

This is why I'm a big proponent of continually telling people on my team what they are good at, even if they already know it. Actually, *especially* if they already know it. Why? Because it's so easy for people to start doubting their strengths. Even though they are gifted, they are not perfect—and sometimes it's the mistakes and limitations that shout at them the loudest. They need a reassuring voice from someone they trust that confirms their calling and ability. If they begin to doubt who they are, they'll stop attempting great things; but if their self-confidence is healthy, they will tackle challenges with courage, faith, and persistence. Instead of playing not to lose, they'll play to win.

Dr. Bandura makes another observation that is particularly relevant to self-leadership. Notice the connection he highlights between self-efficacy and what you allow to occupy your mind.

Those who judge themselves inefficacious in coping with environmental demands dwell on their personal deficiencies and imagine potential difficulties as

48

more formidable than they really are. . . . Such self-referent misgivings create stress and impair performance by diverting attention from how best to proceed with the undertaking to concerns over failings and mishaps. In contrast, persons who have a strong sense of efficacy deploy their attention and effort to the demands of the situation and are spurred to greater effort by obstacles.[8]

This principle is profoundly important. Self-doubt is self-defeating. It creates a negative mental cycle in which each weakness or obstacle you face confirms what you already feared: that you will fail. This inner stress distracts the mind from accessing resources that could address the problem, and that distraction can result in poor decisions. Fear of failure, left unchecked, becomes a self-fulfilling prophecy.

The opposite, however, is also true. Self-efficacy, in and of itself, creates a strong advantage. Even if you are not the most qualitied person in the room, if you have healthy self-efficacy, you will tend to be more successful than those who don't. You will go into situations believing you can succeed, assuming you can figure things out, and knowing you are capable of learning and adapting. Those beliefs will keep you focused on the task ahead rather than wasting emotional energy fighting negative self-talk.

Just to clarify, self-efficacy is very different from self-delusion or foolish pride. Telling yourself you can fly and then leaping off a tall building will not end well, obviously. In the same way, just telling yourself you are good at something isn't going to make you miraculously capable. Similarly, self-efficacy is not an excuse to disregard the voices that speak wisdom into your life. Receiving counsel and advice is essential for every human being, especially leaders. Self-efficacy is simply a humble and settled belief in what's true about your gifts and strengths, of what's in your wheelhouse. It's a belief that, even though you aren't perfect in a particular area, you are skilled and capable enough to accomplish the tasks you face.

Five Essential Self-Efficacy Beliefs

Regardless of whether you call it self-efficacy, self-confidence, or self-love, the principle is clear.

In that vein, here are five beliefs that should be part of every leader's self-efficacy arsenal. Keep in mind, these statements are not grandiose, absolute truths, and some of them might be a work in progress. Balance confidence with humility as you apply them, especially if you are just starting out in leadership. But regardless of the degree to which they are tangibly present in your life so far, they are important beliefs you can use to counter the self-defeating self-talk, and they are worth repeating to yourself regularly.

You will lead yourself better if you first believe in and value yourself.

1. More People Are for Me than Against Me

It's too easy to let a few negative voices or circumstances color your entire outlook. When I wrote my book *Unreasonable Hope*, my agent gave me some wise advice. She said I would see many online reviews, and most would be positive. But, she cautioned, a few would be negative, and those would be the ones that would stick with me. "Don't let a few critics discourage you," she said. "Remember, there are more people for the book than against it." Her warning helped me keep my emotions and thoughts in check over the next few months, because it is human nature to fixate on the negative over the positive—even when the feedback we receive is primarily positive. As a leader, remind yourself that more people are for you than against you. More people are on your side, more people want you to succeed, more people believe in you and trust you. Don't let a few critics and naysayers erase from your mind all the good that is happening.

2. People Like Me

I once heard someone say, "I've decided to believe that everyone likes me unless they tell me otherwise." I think that's a wise philosophy. It's so easy to take every sideways comment or joke as proof that yet another person is against you. Remember the old nursery rhyme, "Nobody likes me, everybody hates me, guess I'll eat some worms"? Don't adopt that as a leadership philosophy. Or a diet, for that matter. Even mean people are rarely trying to be your enemy: actually, they probably don't think about you that much. If you can give them and others the benefit of the doubt, they may eventually become your friends.

3. I Have Nothing to Prove

Believing you have nothing to prove stems from the assurance that whether you succeed or fail, your value as a person remains unchanged. This goes back to understanding the source of your worth, which is your identity as a person, independent of anything else. Your work might be incredible, or it might be terrible, but neither would change your value. Therefore, you don't have to prove your worth to anyone. You should do your work as well as you can, of course, for multiple and obvious reasons. But your work is not a verdict about your worth.

4. Things Are Better with Me, Not without Me

You have something to offer, and you add value wherever you go. Maybe you don't hear a lot of gratitude from those you are helping, but that doesn't change the fact that your contributions are necessary—and probably more appreciated than you realize. If you weren't there, something essential would be missing. You might not always *feel* like this is true, but emotions are notoriously unreliable. Remind yourself how much you matter to those around you.

Meanwhile, be intentional about adding value to people and situations as you are able. Maybe you don't feel like things are better with you around because you haven't been proactive about making them better, and you haven't been proactive because you feel like you don't have anything to offer. It's a self-defeating cycle. Keep reminding yourself you *do* have a lot to offer, then add value as you are able, celebrating the part you are able to play. You are more needed—and you have more to give—than you might realize.

5. I Have Influence

People learn from you, listen to you, and follow you. You are making a difference in their lives. Your influence might be subtle, and it might happen over the long haul, but it is real. And as you look for more ways to use the influence you already have for good, you'll be surprised at the positive effect you can have on others and at how your influence begins to grow.

ooo

What you say to yourself and think about yourself matters, not just on the tennis courts or golf course, but in life and in leadership. Terms such as *self-talk*, *self-image*, *self-love*, *self-efficacy*, and *self-confidence* are far from being self-centered—they simply highlight the premise that healthy leadership starts with you and then extends to others. If you want to lead and serve others better, learn how to shape your thoughts, words, and confidence to empower your efforts, not to discourage them. Believe the best about yourself, then do your best to live up to your own expectations.

KEY TAKEAWAY

How you see yourself and how you talk to yourself have a direct influence on your success, your influence, and your leadership.

SIX

Awkward Is a Gift

Sebastian Thrun is, in his own words, "an odd bird." When he was in his early teens, he spent nearly every afternoon alone in his room, programming and reprogramming a Texas Instruments TI-57 calculator that reset itself every time it was turned off. "It has fifty steps, so it memorizes keystrokes. And I programmed video games. I programmed geometric calculations and all kinds of stuff," he recalls in a CNBC interview. "Maybe I'm socially challenged or what have you. But at a time when computers weren't used by anybody, I came across this programmable calculator . . . And I developed a passion for lying in bed and just figuring out what can you do with fifty programming steps."[1]

Sebastian's passion for innovation and technology soon became more than a passing hobby. When he was eighteen, his best friend died tragically in a car accident. That's when Sebastian began to dream about inventing a car that could drive itself in order to save lives needlessly lost to human error. He went on to earn a PhD in computer science and statistics from the University of Bonn in Germany, and then to become a tenured professor at Stanford. At Stanford, his dream came true: he built a self-driving car that won the 2005 DARPA Grand Challenge, a 130-mile course across the Mojave Desert with a $2 million prize. Sebastian later helped found and lead Google X, Google's top-secret research lab that created their self-driving cars. It was Sebastian who approached Google founder Larry

Page with the vision to photograph every street in the world, better known today as Google Street View.

Sebastian's list of projects, inventions, and initiatives is impressive, but he eventually discovered a passion beyond simply innovating in technology: educating others in technology-related fields. In 2012, he left his high-paying career to start Udacity, an online platform dedicated to bringing tech educational programs to people who otherwise would not have access to them. And he didn't do it for the money or even the prestige. "I could be running possibly the coolest lab on the planet," he said, "and here I am, giving up 97 percent of my salary."[2] He sums up his vision this way: "I have this dream that if we can make education globally, universally available—it doesn't matter if you live in the Middle East, or in South America, you get the same education everywhere—then we can completely transform the world."[3]

"Junior high geek" sounds more like a sitcom cliché than a description of a man who would eventually become a world-changing scientist, inventor, and educator. What took Sebastian from awkward to influential? Many things certainly contributed: innate ability, intelligence, hard work, being in the right place at the right time, and more. But one particular statement he made in an interview stood out to me. When asked to name the last time he felt dumb, he said, "Today, talking to some of our students here, I realized they are smarter than me." Then he added, "But I love feeling dumb."[4]

Part of self-leadership is accepting that you do not have to be perfect to be a leader.

That short statement says so much. It's a window into how a creative, innovative leader thinks and how he processes his own deficiencies or awkwardness. Every leader feels dumb at times, but what you do with that feeling has the potential to make or break your leadership. Once in a while (maybe frequently), you will feel awkward, like a misfit, like you don't measure up to expectations. That is okay. It's actually a gift, if you know how to handle it correctly. Can you imagine how much healthier, how much more fun and relaxed, and how much more empowering leadership would be if we could all learn to *enjoy* the feeling of not being the smartest person in the room, rather than feeling *threatened* by it?

I'm not saying you don't have to grow or change, either, but you are who you are. You can't completely change that, and you shouldn't try. Rather, you should lean in to the uniqueness of who you were made to be. Your "odd bird" passions and your "feeling dumb" moments simply remind you of your uniqueness.

So how is awkward a gift? (And remember, by "awkward" I mean the ways you don't fit the mold: your quirkiness, your nerdiness, and even your shortcomings . . . or at least your shortcomings as defined by your expectations or the expectations of others.) Awkward can be a gift for one of two reasons: it can point to areas in which you are uniquely gifted, like Sebastian Thrun and his propensity for technology; and it can highlight genuine areas of lack where you need to either improve or bring others alongside you. Either way, being awkward is not something to fear, resent, or—worst of all—hide. Instead, acknowledge it. Lean into it. Learn from it. Let it help guide what you focus on or what you choose to leave for someone else.

You can only do so much; you can only be good at so many things. Discover what you are good at or could be good at, what you like, what drives you. Then leverage who you are to accomplish what only you can accomplish. You'll never be successful at being somebody else, but you certainly can become a better version of you. And along the way, your honesty and willingness to staff your weaknesses will help others step into their potential as well.

Inferiority Complex

Being comfortable with your awkwardness is easier said than done. We might applaud Sebastian Thrun for embracing situations in which he feels dumb, but we would still prefer to avoid those moments at all costs. Why? Often, it's because we struggle with feelings of inferiority. We secretly fear we aren't enough, and feeling dumb seems like the last thing we need. We long to feel capable, successful, sufficient—and our inner lack of peace makes embracing awkwardness hard to do.

It was French psychologist Alfred Adler who first coined the term "inferiority complex" in the 1920s. He suggested that, since we are born into a world of adults, we start life knowing that we are smaller and weaker than those around us. He believed that these feelings should motivate us, in a positive way, toward personal growth and superior goals. However, some individuals aren't able to get past the sense that they are smaller and weaker than those around them. Their feelings of inadequacy are amplified over time by perceived failures and frustrations, and they ultimately become crippling, which results in what Dr. Adler called an inferiority complex.[5]

Today, the term has become part of our everyday language, and we use it to describe a wider range of feelings than Dr. Adler's original definition probably intended. Feeling inferior is a matter of degrees, and we all experience it to one degree or another. At some point, in some area, we hear the voices of inferiority, insecurity, and inadequacy whisper in our ears, trying to convince us that we aren't enough for the task at hand or for the challenges ahead. Of course, as Adler taught, we can mature and grow beyond such self-defeating thoughts, but that's often easier said than done.

I consider myself a fairly secure person, but one of my first experiences as a new California resident reminded me how easily feelings of insecurity can strike. My wife and I had moved to Los Angeles from a relatively small town in Washington State. We were used to the casual, unassuming lifestyle and dress of the Pacific Northwest, the polar opposite of Hollywood glamour.

One night, we ate dinner at a restaurant in Malibu Beach known for being frequented by celebrities. I remember looking around at a room full of the most beautiful, elegant, well-dressed, and seemingly self-assured people I had ever seen and feeling completely out of my element. At that moment, I had to make a conscious decision not to listen to the voices in my head that told me I had nothing to offer, that no one in the entire state of California would listen to me. I had to choose to focus on who I was, not who I was not; on what I had to offer others, not on how I could compete with them; on what I thought of me, not what they thought of me. Within a few seconds, my mind stopped feeding me insecurities and instead started rehearsing the unique experiences and knowledge and values we brought with us.

It was a healthy experience, actually, because it reminded me that it's okay—actually, *essential*—to simply be myself. That simple realization took the anxiety level down to zero and allowed me to enjoy the evening.

To this day, that restaurant is one of our favorite places to go. And when we are there, I still look around the room in awe—but it's the awe of admiration, not intimidation.

The key to handling those feelings of not fitting in, of not measuring up, of feeling awkward and out of place, is to just be you. Humbly accept what you are not, but let those feelings also remind you of what you *are*. The areas where you are "weird" or a "nerd," where you obsess, where you find yourself internally motivated to study and experiment and learn—are often areas where you are particularly gifted to think and lead beyond most people. In a sense, everyone is awkward, because everyone is unique. That is a realization as beautiful as it is necessary.

The Comparison Trap

In order to see awkwardness as beautiful, though, you'll have to learn how to recognize and avoid what is maybe the greatest single obstacle to being comfortable in your own skin: comparison. Comparison is the root of feelings of inferiority and insecurity, as Dr. Adler pointed out long ago. At times, you still feel like a kid in an adult world: everyone else is taller, faster, smarter. You compare your worst or your mundane to other people's best. You take note of the parties you weren't invited to, the events at which you weren't asked to speak, the jobs you weren't given. And if you're not careful, you start to draw large-scale conclusions from a few small data points. A handful of failures or underwhelming performances will make you write off entire areas of your life: *I'm not a good public speaker. I'm terrible in social settings. I don't have anything to say. I don't have a sense of humor. People don't like me.*

Comparison locks you up. You have gifts, but if all you listen to are internal voices telling you you're inferior, you'll never value them or use them. You'll even despise them, resent them, bury them. I can think of few things more tragic than potentially great leaders burying their talents because they felt small in comparison to someone else. Pastor and author Craig Groeschel says it this way: "The fastest way to kill something special is to compare it to something else."[6]

lllll

On the other hand, security and confidence are freeing. Security in who you are makes you followable. People love to be around leaders who are comfortable in their own skin, because that attitude releases them to be themselves as well. Keep in mind that confidence comes from security, not the other way around. First you become secure on the inside, then you exude confidence on the outside: confidence in words, confidence in decisions, confidence in social settings, confidence in your calling. Every form of confidence starts with knowing who you are (identity) and valuing who you are (security).

Insecure people sabotage their leadership without even realizing it. They constantly wonder if someone else is more skilled than them or more popular than them. They feel intimidated by the success of their team members, which is counterproductive since the whole point of a team is to accomplish what one person could not. In the process, insecure leaders make everything about themselves. They may not do so intentionally, but it still happens. They somehow manage to turn every occasion and conversation into something that bolsters their own worth and success.

Secure leaders, on the other hand, can remain in the background or stand in the spotlight, and it doesn't change their sense of self-worth at all. Secure people can celebrate others. They are generous with their praise. They share the platform. They don't think *more highly* of themselves than insecure people; they simply think about themselves *less*. They are secure enough in who they are that they can focus the bulk of their attention on their team—and that is precisely what makes them so followable.

Being Good with Being You

So how do you go from comparison to confidence, from insecurity to security, from inferiority to self-acceptance? Put another way: how does awkwardness become a gift? It's a process, not a onetime event, but it's a process you have to choose to engage with. It won't happen by itself. Here are three essential elements of this journey to self-worth.

1. Decide to Value Yourself and Your Gifts Now, Not Later

Use your feelings of awkwardness as a reminder to value yourself now, for who you are, independent of anyone else's opinions or successes. The voices of insecurity and inferiority are nothing but the comparison trap trying to stop your progress.

At that restaurant, I made a choice to believe in myself and value myself rather than trying to prove myself. It was a small thing, but most of life is made up of small things. It is how you choose to see yourself in those little moments, in those opportunities to believe in yourself or to doubt yourself, that end up defining your self-concept.

If you wait to feel good about yourself until you beat one more person, win one more accolade, or achieve one more goal, you'll be waiting a long time. That's precisely the lie of insecurity—that self-acceptance is waiting on the other side of something you must do or fix or become. If you can't accept yourself now, though, you likely never will.

Valuing yourself and your gifts means recognizing how important you are. No one else can do that for you. Your self-worth is your responsibility. Your team members, your spouse, your boss, your friends—none of them can convince you of your value if you don't believe it yourself, and it will exhaust them to try. What you have to offer is valuable, but if you despise it, you'll hide it, squander it, or dilute it.

Choose to place value on what you bring to the table, starting now. Then, over time, continually increase what you have to offer: learn as much as you can, serve wherever you are able, give the most you can give. But don't wait until you reach some nonexistent, rainbow-pot-of-gold moment before you start valuing yourself.

2. Celebrate Other People—Genuinely and Often

Feeling awkward reminds you of the contributions of others—and that's a good thing. Recognize the talents, wins, and growth of others as often and as exuberantly as you can. First, because they need it and deserve it. But second, because it keeps your mind and emotions in a healthy place.

There is something freeing about cheering for other people. Why? Because insecurity typically tries to pull other people *down* in a misguided effort to feel better about itself, every time you choose to lift people *up*, you are taking a stand against insecurity in your own mind and heart.

You are reminding yourself that you don't need to be better than anyone in order to be valuable; that your worth is not based on your accomplishments; that someone else's success doesn't lower your value.

We can all be successful, which means we can all celebrate other people without feeling like it takes something away from us.

Celebrating others also reminds you that other people are not really the competition. Granted, in certain business or athletic scenarios, other people *are* the competition, but I'm not talking about that—I'm talking about the underlying fear or belief that someone else's success somehow diminishes mine. Success is not a finite quantity that must be shared among us all. If it were, then someone else getting a bigger piece of the success pie would mean there is less for me. But that's not how success works.

3. Invest in What You Are Good At

Feeling different or thinking you don't fit in is a reminder that you are unique. That uniqueness needs to be celebrated and even enhanced. The goal isn't to fit in, because to fit in you'd have to be like everyone else. The goal is to be you. So, rather than spending inordinate amounts of time and energy trying to strengthen your weaknesses, lean into the things you're naturally good at or the areas in which you have greatest potential for growth. Don't ignore all your weaknesses, especially if they are hurting you or those around you in some way, but focus most of your efforts on excelling in your areas of strength.

It's okay not to be good at everything. To use yet another sports analogy, most top athletes master only one sport—and often only one position or category within that sport. They might be skilled at other sports and they might enjoy other sports, but at some point, they choose to focus on the one area in which they have the greatest potential. In the same way, in your areas of strength, strive to become a specialist, an expert, an authority. Not to find value or identity in that (because there will always be a more specialized specialist or a more authoritative authority), but simply because those are the areas in which you can grow and give the most.

Comparison is a black hole that sucks up every compliment and accomplishment and only grows bigger and hungrier in the process. When faced with your limitations, decide to lead yourself away from comparison and toward security. Acknowledge where you're weak. Laugh at yourself. Praise people who are strong in those areas. And then, turn toward your strength and work doubly hard at being even better. If you are the numbers girl, be the numbers girl. If you are the book guy, be the book guy. If you are the systems person, be the systems person. Find your strengths, revel in them—and maybe stop being so dramatic about your weaknesses. It doesn't do you or anyone else any good.

oοo

Awkward can be a gift if you use it right. Like Sebastian Thrun, don't be afraid of "feeling dumb," but rather use your awkwardness, your nerdiness, your strengths, and your weaknesses, to direct your efforts. Turn your creativity and innovation toward your potential. Learn, grow, innovate, network, and most of all *give*.

KEY TAKEAWAY

Rather than ignoring or resenting the things that make you different, lean into them, grow in them, and use them to serve others better.

SEVEN

The Emotionally Healthy Leader

Until the 2020 COVID-19 outbreak, the global financial crisis of 2007–2008 was considered by many to be the worst economic period since the Great Depression (1929–1939). It began in the United States with the bursting of the subprime mortgage bubble, part of the banking sector that focuses on higher-risk loans. Within a few months, the economic effects had spread into other market sectors, sparking dramatic losses in the stock market and inflicting havoc on major banks and institutions around the world. The recession didn't just hit banks and big businesses, either. It also affected small and medium-sized businesses, as well as countless individuals and families. Many people lost their savings, their livelihoods, and, along the way, their hopes for the future.

At the height of the crisis, Warren Buffett—one of the most successful investors in the world—wrote an opinion piece in the *New York Times*. He started by stating the obvious: "The financial world is a mess, both in the United States and abroad." But what he wrote next was a surprise: "So . . . I've been buying American stocks."[1]

Seems counterintuitive, doesn't it? Why buy stock when the future is so uncertain, when companies are floundering and investors are panicking? Buffett answered that question next.

Why?
A simple rule dictates my buying: Be fearful when others are greedy, and be greedy when others are fearful. And most certainly, fear is now

widespread, gripping even seasoned investors. To be sure, investors are right to be wary of highly leveraged entities or businesses in weak competitive positions. But fears regarding the long-term prosperity of the nation's many sound companies make no sense. These businesses will indeed suffer earnings hiccups, as they always have. But most major companies will be setting new profit records 5, 10, and 20 years from now.

Let me be clear on one point: I can't predict the short-term movements of the stock market. I haven't the faintest idea as to whether stocks will be higher or lower a month or a year from now. What is likely, however, is that the market will move higher, perhaps substantially so, well before either sentiment or the economy turns up. So if you wait for the robins, spring will be over.[2]

Buffett consistently ranks among the wealthiest individuals in the world, so we would be wise to listen to his advice when it comes to investing. Don't give in to panic, mass hysteria, or the temptation to jump ship, but also don't be swayed by overly optimistic promises that may have been made out of greed. On another occasion, Buffett said, "Success in investing doesn't correlate with IQ. . . . Once you have ordinary intelligence, what you need is the temperament to control the urges that get other people into trouble investing."[3] The same principle shines through both statements: don't let emotions dictate your actions.

> *Wise leaders don't let panic, fear, excitement, surprise, or any other short-term emotion determine their long-term course.*

Buffett's wisdom applies to more than just investing in the stock market. It applies to any future-focused endeavor, including leadership. Why? Because what we are doing as leaders is essentially investing in the future. We are working, planning, building a team, and advancing toward a goal that is still a long way off. We need to stay the course, which means we must know how to process the emotional ups and downs we will experience along the way.

Emotions are important, and they play many roles in our lives: they add flavor and depth to our experiences, they alert us to things that might be wrong, they motivate us to make changes, and more. But emotions are by definition subjective and temporary, and they have no business making decisions of great importance. If my emotions determined whether or not I got out of bed in the morning, I'd probably sleep in at least four days a week. If my emotions decided which of the things on my to-do list I did next, there are a few that would never get crossed off. If my emotions determined how I treated my kids, how I responded to negative feedback, what I ate, what I spent my money on, or any other number of other things, the results would not be pretty. Why? Because emotions are great to have along for the ride, but they shouldn't be driving the car. They are meant to enrich and enhance our lives, not to control them. Buffett saw the importance of controlling our emotional urges in the field of investing, but it's wise advice for every area of life, especially leadership.

Identify and Lead Your Emotions

In order to control your emotions, you need to first *identify* them and then be intentional about leading them rather than following them. The ability to identify emotion is one thing that makes Warren Buffett such a good investor. He notices when fear or other emotions have affected the market, and he refuses to get caught up in the hysteria of the moment. Instead, he leads through the emotions by making value-based decisions and future-based judgments. He can't control the stock market, but he can control his choices. Inevitably, over time, those principled and non-panicked decisions propel him forward.

As a leader, it's neither possible nor desirable for you to lead *without* emotions. You're not a robot. You are a human leading other humans, and emotions are intertwined in everything humans say and do. Trying to divorce yourself of all feelings would be both damaging and boring. Instead, put your energy into *identifying* your emotions and then *leading* your emotions.

Leaders who can't control their emotions are, in a sense, emotionally immature. They might be organizational giants, but they are emotional toddlers. One of the defining characteristics of toddlers is extreme emotions: they can go from hysterical laughter to maniacal rage to angelic slumber in a matter of moments. That's understandable in children. But when an adult manifests the emotional instability of a child, something is wrong, and someone is going to get hurt. And the hurt is only magnified when that adult is also a leader, because a leader has even greater influence.

Emotionally unstable leaders have power, but they don't have the self-control needed to manage that power in difficult moments. If they are unduly controlled by things such as fear or anger, they easily misuse their power. For example, emotionally unstable leaders might fire a valuable employee in a moment of rage. They might make rash decisions that affect the whole organization, such as shutting down a department or selling out to the competition. They might use their platform to make public statements that spread fear or defame individuals. They aren't necessarily bad people, and they don't necessarily have evil intentions—but because they can't control their reactions, they end up making decisions that are ill-advised, irrational, and at times even illegal or immoral.

The problem is, we can often hide our emotional instability behind organizational or leadership strengths. If we speak well in public, make generally good decisions, motivate people, raise funds, win arguments, negotiate, delegate, organize, create good products, brainstorm new ideas, envision the future, or do a good job at any of the other things leaders do, we will likely be considered a good leader. But if we can't identify when we are upset or fearful and control our reactions, we will inevitably end up sabotaging our leadership and hurting those we lead. An emotionally weak leader is a weak leader. Period.

> *Emotionally mature leaders identify those emotions for what they are and then lead themselves out of instability.*

Emotional instability has an especially negative effect on decisions and relationships, two of the most important things a leader must protect. Leaders who are emotional toddlers tend to respond to stress by making hasty decisions, correcting people harshly, giving up on projects prematurely, posting nasty blogs, firing people on impulse, and lashing out at family members or team members.

They grab a nap or a sandwich, decompress, and then face the situation from a more stable place.

All of us have been in seasons and settings in which we gave in to our emotions, and we know the feelings of regret that follow. We realize, after the fact, *I reacted out of my emotions. I spoke out of my fear and stress. My anger got the best of me.* I'm not talking about a passionate personality; I'm talking about emotional instability. Emotional instability is what causes us to spend money we shouldn't spend, eat things we shouldn't eat, talk in ways we would normally never talk, flirt with someone we should stay away from, and ultimately live in a world of regret because we can't identify and lead our emotions.

The key to leading yourself in this area is to be intentional about understanding your emotional makeup, and then choosing to control your emotions so your emotions don't control you.

How to Identify and Lead Your Emotions

It's surprisingly difficult to navigate emotions, as any couple who has had a late-night fight that seemingly came out of nowhere can attest. Our emotions are deeply intertwined with everything we think, say, and do, and sometimes it's hard to know if it's our brain talking or our fear and hurt. To complicate things even more, emotions can be influenced by countless factors ranging from hunger to hormones. It can feel like a challenge just to stay emotionally stable in our personal and family life, not to mention being emotionally healthy as a *leader*. Admittedly, it's not easy, but it's also not impossible. Here are a few questions I encourage you to ask yourself on your journey to emotional strength and stability.

1. What Is My Go-To Dysfunction?

Your go-to dysfunction is the negative and perhaps even destructive behavior that indicates your emotional state is not where it should be. Everyone has one—or more—of these dysfunctions, but not everyone admits it. If you're not sure what yours is, just ask your spouse, your friends, or the people you work with every day, and they can probably tell you! How do you start to break down under pressure? What sort of destructive

66

behavior are you prone to? Put another way, when you lose it, what does it look like? Those might sound like depressing questions, but identifying your tendencies under pressure is actually a positive, wise, and proactive step toward keeping your emotional ups and downs from hurting people.

There's a reason new vehicle models go through numerous crash tests before they hit the market. Engineers want to determine potential points of failure with a couple of crash dummies rather than putting human lives in danger. Based on the results of those tests, they improve their product proactively.

You might not be able to practice your leadership on crash dummies, but you can look at how you've "crashed" in the past—that is, how you've reacted when stressed. Do you shut down? Do you lash out? Do you blow up? Do you give up? Do you look for an escape, maybe through substance abuse or other self-destructive behavior? Do you make rash decisions? Do you run away? Do you get depressed? Do you have panic attacks? Do you binge-watch entire seasons of reality shows while eating deep-fried Oreos and posting depressing memes on social media?

No one wants to think they are "acting too emotional" or "getting carried away," but we all do it from time to time. If you can learn to identify the signs that your emotions have hijacked your thoughts, you'll be able to adjust your actions and words accordingly. You'll know when to dismiss the meeting and go play a round of golf, for example, or when to delegate a task to someone else.

Again, there is no shame is identifying your dysfunction—that is actually bravery, humility, and honestly. The biggest mistake would be hiding or ignoring your dysfunction until it hurts someone when stress gets the best of you.

2. What Triggers My Emotional Dysfunctions?

Once you've identified what your go-to dysfunctions look like, start thinking about what tends to trigger that behavior. What circumstances or factors turn you toward the "dark side"? Think back on times when your emotions have gotten the best of you and take note of any patterns. Leading yourself starts with knowing yourself, and part of knowing yourself is understanding the external factors that could be affecting you internally. Some factors might be specific to you and your situation, but many are probably the same things that tend to affect all of us negatively. What are some of these factors?

To start with, *unmet or urgent physical needs can trigger emotional instability.* These include tiredness, hunger, hormones, stress, illness, and chronic pain, to name a few. For example, if you skipped breakfast, ate only a bag of chips for lunch, and find yourself experiencing an apocalyptic meltdown at 4:00 p.m. because the photocopier jammed again, your emotions and your body might be trying to get your attention. Snickers did a whole advertising campaign about how you're not you when you're hungry. The pop-culture term "hangry" exists for a reason—we've all felt hunger-induced anger. Don't blame the copier. Just get some food in your system.

Because hunger, exhaustion, and other physical factors can wreak havoc on your emotional state, one of the healthiest things you can do for yourself and your team is to take care of your physical needs and habits, especially in areas such as diet, rest, and stress management. Your team needs you to be fully you—the rested, happy, stable, balanced, joke-cracking, grace-giving you—not some emotionally distraught, pessimistic version of yourself. For example, consider ignoring your email inbox at night, picking up a hobby, eating breakfast rather than just inhaling a triple latte at stoplights, taking up yoga, or working from home a couple days a week. All of this is up to you: no one else can control your habits and schedule.

Stress, loss, and trauma, especially over the long term, can also trigger emotional issues. We can't avoid these things, but we can learn how to process them in a healthy way. If you've gone through a traumatic experience, if you've lost a loved one, if you and your spouse are having a lot of conflict, if you're under a lot of pressure—whatever it is, don't be embarrassed to ask for help. We've all done it, or at least we all should. Find a therapist, a coach, or a support group; connect with individuals or a community where you can be honest with your feelings and find genuine help. Get healthy on the inside so you can lead from a place of strength.

Finally, *difficult circumstances can trigger emotional issues.* The stress and anxiety associated with factors beyond our control have a way of wearing us down, and sometimes we don't realize what is happening. If you find yourself becoming chronically dark, pessimistic, and negative, take stock of the stressors in your life. Maybe you are facing a lot of problems at once. Maybe you are at risk of losing something valuable. Maybe you are about to let people down who depend on you. Those things are not to be taken lightly—they tend to come out in your tone, in your facial expressions, and in how you treat those around you. While you might not be able to change the circumstances (which is precisely why you are anxious), you can recognize that you are *not* yourself right now, and you can show yourself and those around you some grace.

3. What Are Some Practical Ways I Can Lead My Emotions?

Once you've identified your go-to dysfunctions and what triggers them, you'll be better positioned to lead your emotions. This is essentially a question of wisdom: determine the practical things you can do to stay ahead of your feelings.

I've realized that when I feel emotionally triggered in the evening, I usually need a glass of water and a good night's rest. I know that what I'm going to feel at seven o'clock in the morning will probably be completely different from what I feel at ten o'clock at night. So rather than taking my emotions at face value or trying to solve everything in the moment, I simply shelve decisions, problems, and the emotions themselves for the night and reevaluate in the morning. It's a simple step, and it's one that is very personal. Maybe for you, mornings are actually the darkest part of your day and you work best late at night. That's fine—just know yourself.

I've also discovered that exercise helps bring emotional stability. For me, that usually takes the form of basketball or golf. Science tells us exercise triggers the release of endorphins that help counteract the adrenaline of intense emotions. It's a simple but effective (and healthy) strategy to keep your emotions in check.

Rest and exercise are just examples, of course. There is no one-size-fits-all when it comes to maintaining emotional balance. Different temperaments and personalities require different strategies. The important thing is to be aware of your emotional tendencies when you are under stress and take care to control your emotions, rather than being controlled by them.

ooo

Throughout your leadership journey, you'll need more than skill and talent to keep your balance. You'll need mental fortitude. You'll need emotional strength. You'll need to know how to stay calm when "fear is widespread," as Warren Buffett wrote during the recession, knowing that your leadership investments will pay off if you keep your head and stay the course.

Learning to lead your emotions is a journey of self-awareness and self-control, of social skills and relationship management. It's not easy, but it's not impossible either. Learn how to maintain emotional health and stability, how to believe in the future even when the present seems shaky and uncertain. And, most important, learn how to love and serve the people around you no matter what.

KEY TAKEAWAY

Learn to know, understand, and lead your emotions through the ups and downs of life.

EIGHT

Don't Break Your Stride

A few years ago, John G. Roberts Jr., chief justice of the Supreme Court, was asked to deliver the commencement address at his son's ninth-grade graduation ceremony. He gave the usual words of greeting, gratitude, and inspiration, but his speech then took an unexpected turn. Commencement speakers, he told his audience, typically wish the graduating class good luck, but he was not going to do that. Then he explained why:

> From time to time in the years to come, I hope you will be treated unfairly, so that you will come to learn the value of justice.
>
> I hope that you will suffer betrayal, because that will teach you the importance of loyalty.
>
> Sorry to say, but I hope you will be lonely from time to time, so that you won't take friends for granted.
>
> I wish you bad luck—again, from time to time—so that you will be conscious of the role of chance in life and understand that your success is not completely deserved, and that the failure of others is not completely deserved, either.
>
> And when you lose, as you will from time to time, I hope every now and then your opponent will gloat over your failure. It is a way for you to understand the importance of sportsmanship.

I hope you'll be ignored so you'll know the importance of listening to others.

And I hope you will have just enough pain to learn compassion.

Whether I wish these things or not, they're going to happen. And whether you benefit from them or not will depend on your ability to see the message in your misfortunes.[1]

I'm not sure if a graduating class of middle school boys fully appreciated his words, but there is a lot of wisdom in them.

Life isn't always easy, but how we choose to respond to misfortunes can make all the difference. Part of learning to lead yourself is realizing that you have two choices when you encounter a negative situation: you can resent it and just try to survive, or you can accept it, learn from it, and come out stronger.

For me, stride represents your forward momentum. It is part attitude, part courage, part faith, and part stubbornness. More than anything, not breaking your stride means refusing to let obstacles stop you.

Don't let anything break your stride.

If you've seen a running back in the NFL tuck the football to his chest and plow, push, and pivot his way through a defensive line, you know what it means to not let anything break your stride. Good running backs never stop churning their legs, no matter what. They don't care that a living wall of enormous humans is intent on dragging them down. They expect that. In fact, they thrive on it.

One of the stats that matters most for running backs is "yards after contact," which refers to the distance players run *after* a player from the opposing team first touches them. Anyone can seem tough when they are first handed the ball, but it's what a player does and how far he goes *after* contact that separates the great running backs from the average ones. A similar principle applies in leadership. All leaders have to battle through some form of resistance or opposition—that's a given. What matters most is how we respond after first contact with that wall.

One of the best things you can do to overcome the resistance or obstacles you'll face in leadership is to prepare yourself before the obstacles come. You do that by deciding ahead of time that you are not going to give up easily, that you are not a quitter. Even if people quit on you, even if life throws something unexpected at you, even if you fall and get up and fall again, you're not going to stop. Your leadership legs will never stop churning. Try to foresee what things could break your stride and pivot around them. Learn from the things that stopped you in the past and be better prepared next time.

What Breaks Your Stride?

Not breaking stride means that, over the long haul, you consistently make forward progress. It's a mindset focused on the long-term. Short-term obstacles won't derail you if you're determined to keep moving toward your long-term goals. Leaders who keep their stride are leaders who are committed to staying the course.

Usually, your stride tends to be broken by something specific, not just by the general wear and tear of life. If you've ever gone on a run through a park or across a field only to trip on a random rock in your path, you know the feeling of having your stride (and maybe your ankle) broken by something unexpected. It's dramatic, it's jarring, and it's painful.

> *Even if their stride is temporarily interrupted by something, leaders find a way to get back to their pace.*

In the same way, there are specific areas or instances that can cause us to break our stride as leaders. Below are four of the main areas that I have observed. If you remain aware of these as you continue down your leadership path, you're much more likely to avoid tripping over them.

1. Relational Conflict

Some degree of conflict is inevitable when imperfect human beings work together. It's not the presence of conflict that threatens to break your stride, but your ability to process it in a healthy way. It's hard to advance when you're facing conflict in your family or when team members aren't getting along. It's hard to focus on the future when hurt, regret, or bitterness keep

73

your mind trained on the past. While there is no one-size-fits-all solution to relational conflict, you can decide to be the kind of person who engages and works through those issues rather than allowing them to stop your forward progress.

2. Financial Pressures

As with relational difficulties, financial challenges are part of life for most of us, at least from time to time. Lack of money can be a genuine and frustrating hindrance to advancement. However, while financial issues are real, money does not have to have the final say in your leadership. You will rarely have a budget big enough to do everything that is in your heart or written on the whiteboard in your conference room. If you do, maybe you need a bigger whiteboard! But a financial limit, like any challenge, isn't automatically a bad thing. In fact, it can spur creativity and focus. It can cause you to be more efficient. It can make you ask hard questions that needed to be asked anyway, such as whether or not a certain program, project, or position needs to be adjusted in some way. How you choose to face your financial pressures is a key part of not breaking stride. Stay grounded, stay objective, stay positive. Even if you have to make cuts or sacrifices, even if you don't know what the future holds (and no one does), don't allow panic to set in. It never helps.

3. Unexpected Circumstances

Some circumstances in life are expected, or at least give some advance warning. For example, you have nine months to prepare for a new baby. That's not nearly enough, as any new parent will tell you, but at least you know it's coming. Other circumstances, whether positive or negative, arrive unannounced, such as a sudden job change or an illness.

Change is rarely easy, and yet life is full of changes. In the 1960s, psychiatrists Thomas Holmes and Richard Rahe hypothesized that any life event—desirable or undesirable—that requires significant change is inherently stressful. They developed a tool called the Social Readjustment Rating Scale that ranked various events according to the degree of readjustment required and the corresponding stress level produced in participants. They identified a whopping forty-three different life changes that people commonly face.[2] And since stress is cumulative, if you're facing multiple changes at the same time, you are going to feel the weight of all of those at once.

Bottom line: change is normal, and it usually involves some level of stress, so you need to get used to dealing with it. Just because life changes doesn't mean you have to break your stride. You can *adjust* your stride, establish a new normal, and find ways to continue moving forward. It might take a little while to gain momentum again, but you will, because it's your stride. It's who you are, it's what you do, it's how you roll. If loss has derailed you, grieve in a healthy way, but don't live there forever. I say that carefully, because some losses live with us for a long time—but even so, they don't have to paralyze us. Avoid cultivating resentment toward whatever life has thrown your way, and don't be angry when you face obstacles or resistance in the future. Instead, focus on adjusting to every new stage and learning to take steps forward again.

4. Moral Failure

For me, moral failure refers to an action that violates widely held standards that a person is reasonably expected to fulfill. I'm not referring to moral gray areas or issues of personal conviction, but rather to significant breaches of integrity. Historically, if you look at the impact of moral decisions by key leaders, especially leaders in the public eye, you'll realize that morality matters in every area of life—in your marriage and family, in your finances, in your communication, and in everything you do as a leader. And who you are and what you do in one arena can't help but permeate every other arena, which is why moral failure can have such an effect on your leadership stride.

If you have unresolved moral issues—words and behaviors that have compromised your integrity—it's likely you've experienced some break in your stride. Exercise self-leadership by addressing whatever it is directly. Recognize the problem, apologize, and make amends where possible. Take time to deal with any issues underlying your failure. Did you lie because you were afraid? Lash out because you felt vulnerable? Make poor choices because you were in pain? Find help, find healing, find forgiveness—but don't withdraw from life.

If you have not compromised your moral integrity but you are facing the opportunity or temptation to do so, please consider the long-term consequences. Look for the third option—the one that doesn't involve moral compromise, but that deals with whatever short-term conflicts are pushing you toward regrettable decisions. Whether that means addiction counseling, marriage counseling, organizational restructuring, sabbaticals, or any other number of steps that can address the immediate hardship or pain, all of those are preferable to making a choice you might regret for the rest of your life.

These four things—relational conflict, financial pressure, unexpected circumstances, and moral failure—are some of the main obstacles that could break your stride, but there are others. As you move through life, keep an eye on your stride, on your pace of forward progress, and learn to identify (and avoid) specific issues that could trip you up.

Choose Your Mindset

Not breaking your stride in leadership is often a question of attitude rather than circumstances. That is, what matters even more than the issue you are facing—including the four mentioned above—is your mental strength and your choice to keep a positive outlook when facing it.

Napoleon Hill, author of the books *Think and Grow Rich* and *Success through a Positive Mental Attitude*, first popularized the idea of PMA—positive mental attitude—as a contributing factor in achievement and success. For Hill, a positive mental attitude is characterized by faith, hope, courage, initiative, generosity, tolerance, and other positive mindsets. These characteristics are not the exclusive property of gifted individuals but rather character qualities anyone can develop. Which means that regardless of your circumstances, your attitude is under your control—you get to choose your mindset. That's the starting point for your PMA.

The term "optimism" is, in many ways, synonymous with PMA. Author and leadership expert Peter Northouse defines *optimism* as "the cognitive process of viewing situations from a positive light and having favorable expectations about the future." He states, "Leaders with optimism are positive about their capabilities and the outcomes they can achieve."[3]

Experts debate whether individuals are optimists or pessimists by nature or by choice, but regardless of your natural bent, your upbringing, or your leadership experience, you can still choose to take a positive point of view. Again, you determine your attitude. And on a related note, you also have a say in whom you surround yourself with. The people in your life and on your team can either promote optimism or fight against it. To the extent you are able, look for positive people, spend time with positive people, hire positive people, promote positive people. Whether you are optimistic, and whether you are surrounded by optimism, depends a great deal on you.

Positive Mental Attitude is one way of describing the power of optimistic thinking, but there are others. In his book *Principle-Centered Leadership*, educator and businessman Stephen Covey conveys a similar idea using the terms *abundance* and *scarcity*. According to Covey, leaders with a scarcity mentality treat life like a zero-sum game: gains and losses have to balance, so one person's gain is another person's loss.[4] In other words, if you have this mentality and someone else gains something—praise, a promotion, an opportunity—you would experience it as a personal loss, which creates insecurity and competition because you don't want to lose out. In contrast, if you have an abundance mentality, you would see the gains of others as gains for all—a win-win—and you would be far more open to the contributions and successes of those around you.

When you find yourself struggling with your attitude in a challenging situation, what's your typical mindset? Do you have an abundance mentality or a scarcity mentality? Do you believe a win-win is possible, that there is enough to go around, and that you can work together to find a solution? Or do you feel afraid and defensive, worried that a solution that is a gain for others would be a loss for you? If you find yourself drifting into a scarcity mindset, recognize what is happening and recover an abundance mindset. Remember, you lead yourself—you can determine your attitude and choose to be positive.

I love this statement from basketball legend Michael Jordan, who was one of my childhood heroes:

I've missed over 9,000 shots in my career. I've lost almost 300 games. Twenty-six times I've been trusted to take the game-winning shot and missed. I've failed over and over and over again in my life. And that is why I succeed.[5]

Failure, resistance, lack, loss—they are an inevitable part of the fabric of leadership. But they don't have to stop you. If you can find the "message in your misfortunes," as Justice Roberts said, it may well propel you forward.

KEY TAKEAWAY

Don't let anything break your stride: no matter what you might face, have a positive attitude, adjust as needed, and keep moving forward.

NINE

Becoming Followable

D ries Depoorter is a Belgian digital artist who combines electronics and a dark sense of humor to create installation art and apps that highlight issues such as social identity, surveillance, encryption, and online privacy. One of his art installations, called "Quick Fix," is a coin-operated vending machine that dispenses social media likes and followers. Consisting of little more than a circuit board, a keyboard, and an LCD screen, his wall-mounted machine allows customers to deposit one to three euros, type in their social media handles, and immediately receive an allotted number of likes or followers, all from fake accounts.[1]

The project is a perceptive commentary on the need people feel to increase social media presence. History may well look back on this era and define it as the age of social media. It's impossible to overstate the impact of having instant access to the attention and opinions of so many people. According to data compiled by creative agency We Are Social, nearly half of the world's population—some 3.5 billion people—actively uses social media.[2]

The easily quantifiable nature of social media—numbers of followers, views, likes, comments, reposts, and more—readily lends itself to comparison—and comparison inevitably turns into competition. That is especially true when advertising dollars are at stake. And there are a lot of dollars at stake in today's online economy. Kim Kardashian West said in a court filing, reported by *Business Insider*, that she receives $300,000 to $500,000 for "just a single Instagram post endorsing another company's product that I like."[3]

A beauty blogger, fashion designer, photographer, or influencer who wants to cash in on advertising dollars or make a name for themselves has to have a massive following to stand out among the competition. And that, predictably, has led to the dubious business of buying followers. While the practice is generally frowned upon, it seems to work, at least in some instances, because advertisers still want to see numbers. Social media consultant Anita Hovey told an interviewer, "We've all been trying to change it around, to say that quality matters more than quantity, but there are still so many clients out there that think purely about numbers. People see their reach as a concrete number and base their judgments on that."[4]

In the influencer economy, where people are paid based on their social reach, brands are routinely paying extra to reach followers who don't exist. Security firm Cheq, in conjunction with University of Baltimore economist and professor Roberto Cavazos, conducted extensive analysis on the impact of fake followers in the advertising sector. They concluded that fake influencer marketing cost advertisers $1.3 billion in 2019.[5] They estimate that the cost in 2020 will be higher, some $1.5 billion. Clearly, the issues of fake followers, fake leaders, and fake influence are not going away.

If you want genuine influence, you have to be genuinely followable.

Don't get me wrong: I don't think social media is evil or that all influencers are fraudsters. But the debate and controversy surrounding followers on social media has an important corollary for us as leaders: gaining followers, and therefore gaining influence, is not something that can be forced, faked, or manipulated without consequence. On social media, fake followers are looked down on, not just because it's dishonest and unethical to be paid for nonexistent influence, but also because healthy, authentic influence happens only one way: by being followable. The same thing is true in leadership.

Work on Yourself First

Leaders need to be more concerned with being followable than gaining followers, and I'm not talking about social media accounts here. I'm talking about every area of life and leadership. Being followable simply means that you have what it takes for others to follow you. It means others want to learn from you, imitate you, and work with you.

Becoming followable implies working on yourself first—not on your image or your brand, but on *you*. The real you. The person others will lean on in hard times; the person you are when no one is around. It means developing the skill, character, and knowledge necessary to lead others.

On numerous occasions I've listened to young men describe in detail what they are looking for in their future spouse, and often their list of qualities and qualifications is unrealistic enough to scare off any sensible woman. I usually say something along these lines: "Don't focus on finding the best woman you can. Focus on being the best man, the best future husband, the best future father."

What I *want* to say, but rarely do, would sound more like this: "Bro, first of all, that woman doesn't exist. And second, if she did, God Himself isn't going to trust you with someone like that if you don't have a job or any discernible skills that don't involve video games, because she deserves more than that. Go work on yourself first."

If you ignore who you are and focus solely on gaining influence and followers, you'll be vulnerable to the same temptation Instagram influencers face: to do whatever it takes to inflate your numbers. Authentic influence, however, can't be measured by a number. It can't be reduced to how many people download your podcast, buy your book, attend your seminars, or tag you online. Those may be indicators of influence, but they can never tell the whole story. Influence is a lot more complicated than that. If you are the kind of person people want to follow, the numbers will take care of themselves, your influence will grow, and you'll be able to start your own beauty products line. Well, maybe not the last one, but the first two will generally follow, at least in time.

Focus on being followable, because the responsibility of leading others is no small thing. We've already seen that no leader is perfect, so I'm not talking about taking on a weight that only God Himself could carry. But if you bear the title of leader, you also bear the responsibilities of a leader. Rather than focusing on followers, focus on being the person your future followers will need so that you're prepared when they come along. When you do, you'll find that influence and leadership tend to occur naturally, over time, in an organic and authentic way. And that's the best kind of influence.

Five Characteristics of a Followable Leader

How, then, do you become a more followable leader? Simply stated, you become a followable leader by becoming the kind of leader you would want to follow. What do *you* look for in a leader? What do you respect or appreciate? What disappoints or demotivates you? Questions such as these help you become the leader people are looking for.

It's worth noting that you shouldn't try to be the leader people *think* they want, but rather the leader they *need*. Leading isn't about winning popularity or about racking up compliments. It's not about being everyone's best friend. Good leaders learn what their followers need and provide that consistently.

Among all the qualities or characteristics that leaders might display, there are several that stand out as nonnegotiable traits of a truly followable leader. These five qualities have the power to inspire others to trust you, listen to you, and follow you—even when the journey isn't exactly what they expected. Make these a part of your life, and you won't have to worry about finding followers: they'll find you.

1. Integrity

Integrity means you are the same inside and out, publicly and privately, today and next year. It means you don't have double standards. I'm not saying you won't ever change, but even your changes will be authentic and transparent. People have to know they can count on you. Hypocrisy and dishonesty are two of the quickest ways to lose influence. If you mislead people in one area, you lose credibility in every area. Your integrity is your credibility, and your credibility is your leadership currency. When people learn that they can count on your integrity, that allows them to follow you even when they don't fully understand (or agree with) the direction you are going. They will trust you, so they will trust your leadership.

2. Selflessness

Selflessness is having genuine concern for the well-being of others. In leadership, it refers to your desire to serve, help, and give to others, especially the team and organization you lead. Leadership is about serving, not receiving. People will only follow a selfish leader for so long, because they will refuse to link their future to someone who doesn't have their best interests at heart. You can fake altruism for a while but not forever, which is why good leaders are intentional about being aware of their motives and keeping them pure.

Give as much as you can, as often as you can, for as long as you can. That's essentially the job description of a leader in any area of life. And the long-term rewards—loyalty, relationship, team growth, and organizational success—will be well worth the sacrifice.

3. Security

Secure leaders tend to attract followers; insecure leaders tend to repel them. Secure leaders tend to release people in the area of their gifting; insecure leaders often subtly sabotage them. Secure people celebrate the success of their team members; insecure leaders are frequently threatened by it. As a leader, learn to be secure. When you do, you'll create a safe, empowering environment that will attract and keep quality followers.

4. Positivity

Your positive mental attitude will have a profound effect on your influence. Anyone can prophesy doom, gloom, and failure. Anyone can play the devil's advocate. Anyone can list out the reasons a project might fail. But it takes a special mix of courage, faith, and mental strength to consistently maintain hope, and that is something people are looking for in a leader. Positivity isn't always about declaring success in the big things, either. It can be as simple as expressing gratitude, appreciating the small advances, laughing at the funny little things that happen along the way, celebrating anniversaries and milestones, and recognizing the contributions of team members. Good leaders take every opportunity to point out the best in the people and situations they encounter.

5. Consistency

Consistency is directly connected to integrity. If you have integrity, that means your morals and values are constant, not situational. They don't easily change. The result, on a practical level, is consistent leadership. You treat people the same, day after day. You have the same rules, set the same expectations, preach the same vision, and have the same reactions, day in and day out. People learn they can depend on you, which produces that most invaluable leadership commodity: trust.

Leadership expert Peter Northouse writes, "Trust has to do with being predictable or reliable, even in situations that are uncertain. For organizations, leaders built trust by articulating a direction and then consistently implementing the direction even though the vision may have involved a high degree of uncertainty."[6] People need to know the direction isn't going to change on a whim. They need to know that what they are building, whom they are serving, and where they are going is relatively stable. As leaders, there is a lot we can't control in the world around us, but we can be consistent, steady, and trustworthy.

Character Beats Vision

Did you notice that "vision" isn't part of my list of five characteristics? There are two reasons for that. First, vision is a given. If you aren't pursuing a common goal, then you're not going anywhere, and you're not a leader. You might be a manager, but leaders, by definition, are headed somewhere. They have a vision.

Second, vision is secondary to character. As I've analyzed and interviewed well-known leaders, and as I've worked with countless leaders, I've seen time and again that people buy into leaders before they buy into vision. Vision is important, but people trust leaders more than vision. Conversely, they are more disappointed and hurt by leaders than by vision. Vision is, for the most part, static. What makes a vision dynamic is the passion and personality of the leader. Become the character-based leader you should be, and vision will take care of itself.

> *Who you are will always speak the loudest and lead the best.*

Ralph Waldo Emerson wrote, "That which we are, we shall teach, not voluntarily, but involuntarily. Thoughts come into our minds by avenues which we never left open, and thoughts go out of our minds through avenues which we never voluntarily opened. Character teaches over our head."[7] That last phrase—"character teaches over our head"—sums up the power of a leader who is intentional about becoming followable. It's not what you say, what you write, what you teach, what you paint on the wall, or what you tattoo on your shoulder that matters.

KEY TAKEAWAY

Become the kind of leader people want to follow, and influence will take care of itself.

TEN

Who Are You Listening To?

n 2011, the Boeing Company was in a race with rival Airbus to design and supply passenger planes for the commercial airline market. Airbus had recently launched their popular Airbus A320neo and was beginning to encroach on Boeing's territory in some sectors of the market. Faced with time constraints and financial pressures, Boeing decided to modernize the 737, its bestselling jetliner first introduced in 1967, rather than design a new plane from the ground up. They called it the 737 Max.

The first test flight took place in January 2016. The 737 Max received FAA certification in March 2017 and began commercial service just a few months later in May. Boeing already had thousands of orders, and production went into full swing.

Less than eighteen months after commercial flights began, tragedy struck. In October 2018, a 737 Max aircraft owned by Indonesian airline Lion Air crashed into the sea, killing all 189 passengers. While no one knew what caused the crash, initial suspicions focused on a flight control system meant to keep the plane from stalling. Boeing sent out a bulletin alerting airlines to the need for better pilot training on that system.[1] But then a second tragedy occurred. In March 2019, an Ethiopian Airlines 737 Max went down with 157 people on board; again, there were no survivors.

Two disasters involving the same aircraft in less than five months? Something was clearly wrong. Boeing came under considerable scrutiny from the FAA, the media, and the world. Everyone wanted answers. At the same time, airlines who had placed orders for the 737 Max wanted to know when they could expect their jets.

Subsequently, Boeing and its CEO, Dennis Muilenburg, suffered through a series of missteps. When journalist Chris Isidore of *CNN Business* analyzed the company's decisions in the aftermath of the crashes, he concluded that Boeing was "wildly optimistic" about a quick fix and "seemed ignorant of the trouble it would have" getting FAA approval for the solutions they hoped to present. According to Isadore, Boeing misjudged the severity of the problem, missed multiple deadlines, and eventually shut down production with no timeline for restarting. "Costs for Boeing are expected to add up to more than $10 billion," he stated, and "it will take years for Boeing to recover from the problems the plane caused."[2]

Isidore put the blame squarely on the CEO's shoulders. "From the beginning of the 737 Max crisis, Boeing CEO Dennis Muilenburg severely underestimated how much trouble the company faced." It eventually cost Muilenburg his job.

Only time will tell how much Muilenberg himself was truly to blame for Boeing's errors, both before and after the fatal crashes. He is only one person, after all, at the helm of a company that employs over 150,000 people.[3] And yet, as CEO he stood, and then fell, for the entire company. "Boeing has mishandled it all," said Scott Hamilton, an aviation industry consultant, adding that Muilenburg was "the face of Boeing. All that falls under his watch."[4]

As the face of Boeing, Muilenburg bore the consequences of poorly made decisions. But I wonder about the sources behind those decisions. On whose reports did he base his production timelines? Who advised him on how to respond to the initial crash? Who were the engineers who informed his reports to the media, to Congress, and to customers? Important decisions are rarely made by one person. Rather, they are the result of numerous factors and voices all the way up and down the leadership chain. And yet, one person—usually the CEO or another top executive—is often held responsible for the decisions of an entire organization, at least in the public eye.

One of the more sobering truths of leadership is that leaders are ultimately responsible for organizational decisions, but they must depend on the information and advice of countless others on their teams. Once leaders have influence and responsibility for large organizations, they can't have firsthand knowledge of every operation, which means they have to rely on the input, expertise, and opinions of the people who report to them. Therefore, the people they choose to listen to—those who inform them, counsel them, mentor them, and otherwise influence them—matter very much.

As leaders, the people we influence and affect may or may not know the sources of our information, but *we* should. It is our responsibility to make sure those sources are a reliable basis for leadership decisions that affect many people.

People and Motives

As you consider whom you will listen to, there are two important voices to consider: the external, audible voice of other *people*, and the internal, silent voice of your *motives*. The first is fairly obvious, while the second is much more subtle; both of them, however, influence our decisions greatly. Let's look at each in more detail.

1. People

One of your main challenges as a leader is to surround yourself with the right people and listen to them. Much of leadership is about decision-making, but decision-making starts with information and advice. If you have bad counsel, you'll likely make bad decisions; if you have good counsel, you'll likely make good decisions. Leaders have to focus on both ends of the process: getting sound counsel from wise people, then making informed decisions that move the team toward the goal.

It might sound counterintuitive at first, but you can't really blame someone for giving you bad counsel if you follow that counsel and things go south. Why? Because you chose to ask the person for advice, and you chose to follow the advice. Those decisions are on you. That is why it is so important to make sure you have the right people speaking into your life. The first decision you make (and the decision that affects all the other decisions) is the decision about whom you are going to listen to, believe, and be swayed by.

The people you listen to should be those who prove themselves to be trustworthy, emotionally mature, and wise. You should be aware of their tendencies, their personalities, their strengths and weaknesses, their reactions under pressure, their fears, and their goals. This was where Rehoboam went wrong. He listened to a group of peers with no real leadership experience over the counselors who had served his father for decades.

Spend the necessary time to get the right people in the right chairs around the decision-making table. In other words, know whom to consult for different areas of need. This includes not just your team but outside consultants or advisers as well.

> *You need people who can see your blind spots and aren't afraid to tell you about them, but who also respect your leadership.*

You need people who know how to celebrate the positives and deal with the negatives. You need people who are good at what you are bad at and who care about the things you typically forget. You need people who think differently from you do but who share your vision. You need people who are positive but not pushovers; encouraging but not manipulative flatterers; honest but not sharp-tongued; empathetic but not emotional basket cases.

A few summers ago, I had lunch with author and leadership guru Craig Groeschel, who is one of my leadership heroes. I asked him what he'd do if he were my age, and he replied that he would invest in leaders. He encouraged me to take the principles I had been studying and the experiences I had gained in church leadership and make them available to a wider audience. It was that conversation that spurred me to start my podcast, *Leadership Lean In*, and eventually to write this book. Had I not asked for counsel, I doubt I would have felt the urgency or had the courage to take those steps. Craig saw a need, and he saw something in me I didn't see in myself. His words encouraged me to do what I would not have done on my own.

That is precisely the power of good counsel: to help us do things we would not have otherwise done, or to help us avoid mistakes we are about to make. More recently, the church I lead launched a second Sunday meeting location. I had been a part of churches that had done that, and I assumed I knew what I was doing. I was wrong. We survived, but to be honest, we made a lot of avoidable mistakes. After a year or so, we finally did what we should have done from the beginning: we sent our key leaders to learn directly from a couple of churches that were successfully doing what we had attempted. If we had asked for counsel first rather than fumbling along on our own, we probably could have saved ourselves six to nine months of lost work and a few bumps and bruises along the way.

Good leaders listen to the right voices not just when their organization is small, but even more so as it grows. Keep in mind that opinions will multiply with organizational growth. The bigger the organization gets, the more haters and critics you'll have as a leader. When that happens, you might be tempted to withdraw and close ranks. But don't give in to the temptation to make your circle of counselors smaller. Good leaders have a table full of voices of influence. In fact, as your team or organization gets bigger, you'll need tables—plural—because you'll likely be responsible for multiple teams.

2. Motives

"Motives" refers to the inner forces or reasons behind what we do and say. Unlike the easily identifiable voices of the people we listen to, the voice of our motives is often hard to define. Motives hide under the surface; they are intangible and invisible, revealed primarily through the actions they incite. It's hard to know the motives of our own hearts, and it's even harder—maybe impossible—to know the motives of another. And yet, nearly everything we do is based on motives. Even when those motives are unconscious, they are still there, exerting a powerful influence on every aspect of our lives. They are voices that guide our interactions, our decisions, and our leadership.

Your challenge as a leader is to learn to identify the inner voices you are listening to. Why do you do the things you do? Why do you talk, act, think, and spend the way you do? Are you influenced by negative motives such as fear, insecurity, or greed? Or by positive ones such as integrity, excellence, and love? To lead yourself well you have to know yourself,

90

and that includes knowing the motives that influence your decisions. You can justify just about any leadership decision if you try hard enough, but that doesn't make it the right decision, much less a decision made for the right reasons.

Before making a decision, do a motives check. Ask yourself a few questions:

- Why do I want to do this?
- What are my superficial motives, the ones visible at first glance?
- What are my underlying motives, the ones hidden deep inside?

If your motives are primarily selfish—pride, ambition, revenge, fear, lust, and so on—you should mistrust your own heart. When your internal "wisdom" is skewed by self-absorption, self-protection, or self-aggrandizement, your decisions will never work out well in the long run. On the other hand, if you tune in to the selfless motives in your heart—love, kindness, forgiveness, generosity—you'll find it easier to make healthy decisions because you are listening to the right voices.

Human nature being what it is, we are often slow to recognize in ourselves those motives that tend to be hidden or cloaked, such as pride, ambition, and revenge—unless we have a little help. That help often comes in the form of a trusted friend, family member, or team member calling you out; a project or business falling apart and forcing some overdue introspection; or intentional, humble self-evaluation. Again, we're talking about self-leadership, so obviously the ideal scenario is the third one—self-evaluation. But don't discount the first two, either. And if they happen, make sure you don't write off the failures as someone else's fault. Every failure is an invitation to learn some valuable lessons about yourself. Accept the invitation.

Becoming aware of the motives behind your actions, decisions, and words is the only way to make sure you are being led by the right voices. You choose which influences to listen to, which forces to yield to, which urges to give in to. While it's not always easy to keep your motives pure, it is both possible and necessary, because your actions and words will eventually reflect whom you're listening to on the inside.

Balancing the Power of Opinions

Leadership requires balancing the delicate tension of caring enough—but not caring too much—about what people say, think, write, and do. You are leading people, and therefore their opinions matter, especially in the case of the inner circle of advisers we talked about earlier. But you can't let your decisions be swayed by every opinion you hear, because there are as many opinions out there as there are people.

Have you ever heard Aesop's classic fable "The Man, the Boy, and the Donkey"? The story begins with a man and his son walking to market with their donkey. Along the way, someone laughs at them for walking rather than riding, so the son climbs up on the donkey. Someone else criticizes the son for making his father walk, so they switch places. Another person then ridicules the father for riding while the son walks, so they decide to ride together. That, naturally, brings criticism in defense of the poor animal, and so the man and his son eventually decide to carry the donkey between them on a pole. That ridiculous decision makes everyone laugh at them even more. Eventually, the donkey breaks loose, falls into a river, and drowns. The moral? "Please all, and you will please none."[5]

If you don't care what people say, you could become a dictator—cold, selfish, unrelatable. You will likely make bad decisions because you'll be issuing decrees from inside a bubble. But if you care too much about what people say, you could end up overthinking everything, compromising your standards, and making decisions based on who is least likely to be offended. Neither option is a good basis for leadership.

Often this comes down to being confident in your decisions. "If you don't stand for something, you'll fall for anything," goes the old saying. When you know who you are and where you're going, and when you're confident that your decisions have been informed by the right people, you don't have to be swayed by criticism. You are more likely to make wise, empathetic, mature choices, and you're less likely to drown your donkey in a river.

ooo

Listening to the wrong voices can have far-reaching negative consequences for leaders, as the story of Boeing CEO Dennis Muilenburg

92

unfortunately illustrates. That is why *whom* you listen to matters so much. Whether it's the people around the table or the motives inside your head, you choose the voices that influence what you say and do. In every important decision, it's worth taking the time to listen carefully in order to make informed, wise, life-giving choices.

KEY TAKEAWAY

Whom you listen to and who influences your decisions will profoundly affect your leadership, so choose wisely what voices you allow into your leadership.

---

ooo

Leading yourself—whether that means identifying your strengths, accepting your weaknesses, becoming emotionally intelligent, or listening to the right people—is the essential foundation for leading people. But while leadership starts with you, it doesn't end with you. Leadership is about *people*. There are people around you who need what you have and who are waiting to follow you. And if there is one leadership lesson that stands out above the others, it's this: people matter most. In Part 2, we explore what it means to become better at the people part of leadership.

PART 2

PEOPLE MATTER MOST

eadership starts with you because you can't lead others if you can't lead yourself. That's why the chapters in Part 1 focused on self-knowledge, self-leadership, and self-mastery.

But even though leadership starts with you, it isn't all about you.

People can sniff out inauthenticity. They can tell if you are in this for them or merely for you. They might follow a selfish leader for a while, but eventually they'll go somewhere else. The best leaders are not those who command people, but those who serve people, teach people, love people, and empower people.

Leadership is about influence, influence means followers, and followers are people. By definition, no one can be a leader unless they have followers, and those followers are human beings with names, needs, and feelings. You must genuinely believe that people matter most, and then keep that belief at the center of your philosophy and value system.

Your leadership end game can't be you: it must be other people.

Part 2, therefore, is about winning with people—or to use a more common term, *people skills*. Anyone can learn people skills, and everyone should. "Skills" implies something that can be improved and mastered. Good leaders— like good athletes, good musicians, and good teachers—never stop learning. So, whether you consider yourself an introvert or extrovert, whether you are socially skilled or socially awkward, you can always get better at working with people. In the next several chapters, we'll look at practical ways to become a better "people person."

ELEVEN

Everyone's Favorite Topic

ecent scientific research backs up what most of us could have guessed: everyone's favorite topic of conversation is themselves. All it takes is a few minutes listening to people talk or browsing social media to see this played out in real time.

Studies of human conversation show that, on average, 30–40 percent of people's everyday speech is used to relay information about private experiences or personal relationships,[1] and a scientific analysis of Twitter indicated that upward of 80 percent of posts are basically announcements about people's immediate experiences.[2] Researchers from the Harvard University Social Cognitive and Affective Neuroscience Lab state that humans are the only primates that consistently attempt to communicate what they know to others, such as pointing out interesting things or modeling behavior for others to imitate.[3] They add that, by nine months of age, babies already begin attempting to draw attention to things they find important in their environment.

The Harvard study used MRI scans and other tools to analyze precisely what happens in the human brain when people talk about themselves. One group of participants was asked to talk about themselves alone, with no one listening, and another group talked about themselves to a listener. Their brains were monitored during the conversations, and the results showed that sections of the brain associated with self-related thought were activated (as expected), but so were areas of the brain generally associated with reward, pleasure, and motivation. This was true (although to a lesser degree) even when the subjects were talking only to themselves. In other words, talking about ourselves simply feels good—even if no one is listening.

This doesn't mean humanity is hopelessly self-absorbed. Rather, it speaks to our innate need to share life with other people and to be known and needed as individuals within a community. We are hardwired to share what we know, enjoy, fear, or care about with others. We need to belong.

Psychologist Abraham Maslow first proposed his famous hierarchy of needs in a 1934 paper titled, "A Theory of Human Motivation." In it, he listed five categories of needs, and exactly halfway up the list is "love and belonging." It comes right after such basic needs as "safety" (security, employment, financial stability, health) and "physiological needs" (food, shelter, sleep, clothing). In other words, people have an inherent need for connection, friendship, and belonging that is only slightly less powerful than their need for survival and safety.

So, what does all of this science about our need for connection and belonging have to do with leadership? As a leader and a person of influence, you can facilitate environments that meet these human needs by giving people a community, a support system, and a voice. If you understand that people need to belong and to contribute, your leadership will be less about yourself, and your goals will be more about the needs and goals of the people who follow you. You will win with people not by bossing them around, but by building them up, listening to them, and embracing them.

Remember, people skills are about *people*. That should be obvious, but it's surprising how easy it is to think your people skills are about *you*. Sometimes this is done self-disparagingly, and you criticize yourself for not being better at dealing with people or for not being more likeable. Maybe you think you need to be a better conversationalist, better debater, better joke-teller, better dresser; or you need to be more informed, more attractive, more dynamic. It might sound humble to belittle yourself this way, but in reality, it makes the issue of people skills about yourself, which is thinking backward. People skills are about people, not you, which means the best way to improve your people skills is to focus on thinking more about others, not more about yourself.

98

Caring and Connecting

Being a leader who is a people person means caring about people and connecting with people. *Caring* refers to the empathy and love that motivates you to engage with others in the first place, and *connection* refers to the human link that you create with them. Both are important, and together they keep your focus in the right place: on the people you serve.

Be aware that it is possible to *connect with people without caring for them*. Leaders can be skilled at appealing to the desires, dreams, and motivations of their followers and be self-serving the entire time. But leaders who connect without caring are engaging in manipulation, not servant leadership. Leaders who know how to rally the troops and motivate people but who do so without the best interests of their followers at heart aren't truly good at leading people—they're just good at using people.

On the other hand, leaders *who care for people but who don't connect with them* will find it difficult to build forward momentum. These leaders can have the best intentions; they can know what people need; they can desire to make a difference in their world—but if they can't build bridges to people's hearts, they won't be able to lead them or influence them toward a common goal, which is the essence of our definition of leadership.

Both caring and connecting start by deciding to be interested in others. They are not personality traits or magical gifts that you either have or don't have. They are a choice, a conscious effort to bend the arrow of your focus outward toward others rather than inward toward self. How are people around you feeling? What do they need? What are they afraid of? What are they hoping for? What drives them? What excites or discourages them? What are they good or bad at? Where do they hope to be in one, five, or ten years?

As a leader, nothing brings me greater or more lasting joy than seeing people engaged, growing, safe, and fulfilled. Leadership that forgets people is leadership that has disengaged from the very reason it exists. That kind of leadership can't thrive or last, because people are the reason, the means, and the goal of leadership, all in one. What you and your team build together matters, but the team of people doing the building matters more. People—in and of themselves—are the point of leadership.

Having good people skills is not the same thing as being skilled in public speaking, knowing how to lead teams, or being the "life of the party." Those things are more about commanding the attention of a group, whereas being good with people is about your ability to interact with individuals. That should be good news if you're an introvert, because you don't have to light up a room every time you walk in—you can just focus on serving people one at a time. In fact, sometimes I think loud people (like me) actually have to work harder at this because we can hide behind charisma or persona in social settings and rarely talk to individuals on a heart level.

People skills require more than just interacting with individuals, though. You have to be aware of the effect your interaction is having on the people you are with, and you have to make that effect as positive and healthy as possible. It's been said that people will forget what you say and do, but they'll never forget how you made them feel. They might call it your vibe, your energy, or something else, but what they are referring to is what they feel in your presence. Leaders with great people skills know how to add something to the people they connect with by encouraging them, praising them, serving them, or helping them in some way.

In his book *The Great Rivalry*, biographer Dick Leonard tells a story that illustrates this dynamic. He recounts a quote from the memoirs of Jennie Jerome, Winston Churchill's mother, who, within a short span of time, had the opportunity to dine with two prominent British figures (both of whom eventually became prime ministers): Benjamin Disraeli and William Gladstone. She summed up her experiences this way: "When I left the dining room after sitting next to Gladstone, I thought he was the cleverest man in England. But when I sat next to Disraeli, I left feeling that I was the cleverest woman."[4]

If you're aware of your effect on people while you are with them, you can do your best to add value and build confidence through every interaction.

Are you more like Gladstone or Disraeli? How do people feel when they are with you and after they leave? Are they impressed by *you*, or are they more confident in themselves? Do your words and demeanor lower their self-efficacy or boost it? Do they believe that what they say matters or that it makes no difference? Do they believe you want them on the team or that they're not that important? Obviously, you can't control what people think or the perceptions they take away from a conversation.

Being aware of how your words and demeanor make people feel isn't about manipulation but rather about choosing to *care* and then communicating that care through human *connection*. It's about being intentional in how you relate to people, and the result is authentic human connections that facilitate effective servant leadership.

Three Practices for Connecting with People

There's no great mystery to connecting with people; it simply takes some intentionality and a lot of practice. While you can find entire books written on the art of human interaction, here are three simple, easy-to-apply suggestions to instantly connect with people.

1. Learn Names

Names matter because people matter—you are not leading nameless, faceless masses, but individuals. As a leader, you can't have a heart connection with nameless people, and you can't win nameless people to your cause.

Everyone loves to hear their name. You can use terms like *bro, friend, buddy*, and *dude*, but they don't carry the same power as using someone's name. Using names helps people feel known and cared for; conversely, forgetting names can make people feel forgotten or unimportant. Calling someone by the wrong name is a secret fear of most leaders, I'm sure, because it is such an easy and harmful mistake—and because we've all done it.

Some people are blessed with the ability to easily remember names and faces. The rest of us have to work at it. I once heard that if you use someone's name six times in conversation within the first few minutes of meeting them, you'll remember it. I don't know if that's scientifically proven, but it works for me. I meet new people all the time, which is not unusual for a leader in any field. I'm intentional about repeating a person's name during that initial conversation, and this simple habit not only helps me remember their names but also helps the conversation go deeper, beyond the typical "How are you?" and "What do you do?"

2. Put People at Ease

If your goal going into conversations is to help people relax and be comfortable, you'll naturally focus on them rather than yourself. On the other hand, if you concentrate mainly on what people think of you, you'll tend to exude defensiveness, which often puts the other person on edge. That's counterproductive because it separates you and the other person rather than bringing you together in an environment of mutual security. Of course, there are certain meetings or conversations that are confrontational in nature or that require some level of negotiation, so I'm not suggesting that your only goal be to make people feel good. But even difficult conversations can be made easier if you work at creating trust by putting people at ease.

How do you do that? I find that body language and posture are the two biggest keys, closely followed by volume and tone of voice. Sometimes we aren't aware that we're coming across as aggressive or keyed-up. We need to slow down, open up our stance, smile a bit more, and give people an opportunity to relax.

3. Ask More Questions

In a paper exploring the value of question-asking, Harvard researchers concluded, "People spend most of their time during conversations talking about their own viewpoints and tend to self-promote when meeting people for the first time. In contrast, high question-askers—those that probe for information from others—are perceived as more responsive and are better liked." They added: "Our findings suggest that people fail to ask enough questions."[5] In other words, you don't make a good impression on people by talking about your achievements, opinions, or plans, but simply by asking questions. You can't win with people if you make everything about yourself. You might build an audience, but you won't build connection and you won't communicate care.

In every conversation, make it your goal to ask more questions than the other person and to talk more about the other person than yourself. My goal when talking to someone, especially someone I've just met or don't know well, is to find common ground. I want to discover a subject we can "run the ball" with. Do they like sports, food, fashion, or travel? Do they have kids the same age as mine? Do they share the same faith, political views, or taste in coffee? Good questions help you find that common ground.

These suggestions—learn names, set people at ease, and ask more questions—are three simple ways to connect with people and get them talking about the topic that is ultimately most important to them: themselves. Those connections, in turn, will empower you to understand people better and therefore serve them better.

ooo

Everyone has an innate need to belong, to connect to others, and to find their place. When you are intentional about allowing people to express their goals, opinions, and feelings, you validate them as individuals. Your time and attention tell them they matter and their stories matter. If you can build this people skill into your leadership habits, you'll never lack for influence.

KEY TAKEAWAY

Give people a sense of belonging, value, and connection by focusing conversation and attention on them, not on yourself.

TWELVE

A Matter of Manners

The phrase "Manners maketh man" might have found renewed popularity due to the *Kingsman* movies, but it has been around since at least the fifteenth century.[1] Usually, it conveys the idea that your manners reveal who you are. But in its earliest use, the phrase had a broader meaning: that manners are what make us human, and etiquette, politeness, and social graces are defining elements of civilization.[2] Manners are considered part of the foundation of civil society because society is made up of people, and people need each other to survive.

Manners might be an old-fashioned idea, but that doesn't mean they are outdated: manners are timeless. What constitutes good manners can vary a great deal from culture to culture, but courtesy will never go out of style; thoughtfulness will never lose its power; saying please and thank you will never become passé.

The word *manners* refers to how we act or behave around others. It can include our demeanor, our vocabulary, our volume, our actions, or any other number of things we do or say. Manners are public and social: they have to do with our bearing and behavior when we are with other people. People matter, therefore manners matter, because manners describe our dealings with people.

Manners are as necessary now as they were centuries ago, especially if you want to lead and influence others. If you want to win with people, show honor. Show class. Show taste. You lose with people by being rude or mean; you win by elevating your words, actions, and attitude with manners. To paraphrase the old maxim, *manners maketh the leader.* (Granted, it's less alliterative, but at least it's gender inclusive.)

Manners in Action

If manners are so important, what does it mean to have good manners? First, and perhaps most important, *having manners means showing respect for other people.* Manners are a direct, visible expression of how much you esteem those around you. Good manners are a way of acknowledging and valuing people. On the other hand, to have bad manners refers to a lack of respect or awareness toward others. We describe people who habitually demonstrate poor manners with terms such as *rude, mean, impatient, offensive,* or *disrespectful.* Good manners are not a onetime decision or action but a lifestyle of respecting and honoring others. Our thoughtfulness, politeness, and courtesy are external manifestations of an internal choice to value people.

Second, *having manners means recognizing the role other people play in your life.* Every time you say *please,* you acknowledge that you need help; every time you say *thank you,* you recognize that someone else contributed to your success. Every time you say *excuse me* or *sorry,* you affirm that you are part of a larger community and your life is intertwined with the lives of others. Manners keep you grounded as a leader by reminding you of your connections with and dependence on the people around you.

Third, *having manners means handling frustration gracefully.* No one is exempt from moments of impatience and frustration, but how you handle those moments says a lot about you. Pope Francis was attending a recent public event when a woman abruptly grabbed his hand and pulled him toward her. She refused to let go even when the pope tried to pull away. Suddenly, in apparent frustration, he slapped her hand and stormed off. The candid and very human moment was captured on live television, and it caused international furor. One Catholic media outlet called it "the hand swat seen 'round the world."[3] Media everywhere ran headlines about how the pope had slapped a woman, which of course sounds terrible any way you say it. The pope's defenders and critics alike immediately took to social media to express their views of what happened. Why? Because even in moments when frustration or impatience is understandable, leaders are still expected to behave with good manners.

The story doesn't end there, though. The next day, the pope apologized publicly, humbly, and with a clear display of emotion. His response highlighted a fourth characteristic of good manners: *having manners means readily apologizing when you fail or hurt someone.* "Love makes us patient," the pope said in his public statement. "So many times we lose patience, even me, and I apologize for yesterday's bad example."[4] He could have claimed he feared for his safety, or that the woman aggravated his sciatica, or any other number of things. Instead, Pope Francis was honest enough to admit that his reaction was regrettable, and his apology speaks very highly of him.

Fifth, *having manners means engaging in specific, deliberate "acts of class."* An act of class, as I define it, is going above and beyond what is expected to show respect, honor, or gratitude. An act of class is a tangible demonstration of consideration, of kindness, of thoughtfulness. That might mean picking up the check, writing a thank-you card, sending a gift, apologizing, opening the door, leaving a generous tip, making a positive comment, holding the door, volunteering to help out with a task, waiting to talk instead of interrupting, sending a courtesy email, or any other number of small things. Often, it's the details that speak the loudest.

Being classy is the opposite of being common. It is more than just not being rude: it means doing more than just the bare minimum.

Finally, *having manners means treating everyone with honor, all the time.* Sadly, it's often easier to be offensive to those who are close to us—and, ironically, most important to us—simply because we don't feel the need to try as hard to treat them with respect. Another old maxim, "familiarity breeds contempt," expresses that dynamic. We can get so familiar with people that we take them for granted, and we undervalue their feelings and their personhood. Manners aren't just for polite company; they're for every relationship, including your closest ones. This requires emotional health and self-control—not because some people are harder to treat with respect than others (but let's be honest, some are), but because stress, exhaustion, and other physical and emotional pressures can temporarily turn us into rude versions of ourselves. Good manners are not situational or superficial: they are a habit, a way of living, that we strive to follow regardless of who we are with or how we are feeling.

The Basics Matter

To be honest, the four most important manners are the same ones our parents or teachers probably taught us when we were children: *say hi, say please, say thank you,* and *don't interrupt.* While we ideally learned how to employ these habits in our routine dealings with people, they have special meaning when applied to leadership. Let's take a brief look at each one and how they can help you connect with people and serve them better.

1. Say Hi: Greet People

Greeting people is a sign of respect. It is an acknowledgment not just of their presence, but of their value. Whenever you can, take time to greet people personally and warmly. It only takes a few seconds, but it creates a lasting impression. Sometimes as leaders we can be in such a hurry to get to the office, or to get the meeting started, or to get everyone back to work, that we forget the value of engaging with people as *people*, not just workers. This can be as simple as walking slower and noticing the people around you. You might stop for a minute and ask about someone's family, health, job, or hobbies. Find ways to get to know people, to connect with people, a little more each day.

When you walk up to a group, introduce yourself to everyone you don't know. When you see friends and acquaintances, greet them by name. Make eye contact, wave, shake hands, hug, or whatever is appropriate. No matter how busy you are, don't use hurry as an excuse to avoid engaging with people. You can almost always spare two minutes of your time to interact with people. Your willingness to greet others expresses honor and humility, and that goes a long way toward winning with people. It's one of the simplest things you can do to gain more influence, create a more welcoming culture, and build more meaningful connections.

2. Say Please: Make Requests, Not Demands

The word *please* communicates respect; you aren't simply demanding something, but rather you are requesting it politely, even though you are the leader. Most of the time, you can phrase your directives not as top-down orders but as requests. Yes, a request from a leader is somewhat rhetorical—if the requests are directed to people who work for you and the requests are reasonable, it's unlikely they'll say no. But requests preserve the dignity of those under your leadership because they acknowledge that people have free will—they can choose to follow you (or not). They also give people permission to push back or even say no if they have a legitimate reason, but without sounding like they are disobeying your orders when they do so.

You don't necessarily have to use the word *please*, either. *Please* is an attitude more than a formula, and there are many ways to make requests if you are intentional about your wording and tone. For example:

- Would you be able to . . .
- When you have a chance, could you . . .
- Would you mind doing . . .
- What would you think about . . .

There may be times when someone says no or makes an excuse you don't think is valid, and at that point, you might need to overrule the objection and issue a more direct command. But if you have first listened to the objection or opinion, your directive will feel less like an order from a disconnected superior and more like an informed judgment call by a true leader. Most of the time, people will appreciate that and respond well.

3. Say Thank You: Express Gratitude

Writer William Arthur Ward once said, "Feeling gratitude and not expressing it is like wrapping a present and not giving it."[5] Whenever possible, acknowledge people by name and celebrate their contributions. Not only do you build up that person, but you communicate to everyone that you are a team player and that every team member matters. There are few things more motivating to a person than gratitude expressed by a leader, and even more so when that gratitude is expressed in front of their peers. You reassure people that you are not leading from an ivory tower, disconnected and disinterested; rather, you are aware of their sacrifice and grateful for it.

There are many ways to say thank you. I don't have one system or process. In fact, I actually love to think of creative ways to express gratitude, and those depend on the situation and the person. Some of the volunteers in our church are college students, and sometimes they drive me to the airport or help with some errand. They don't expect anything, but I'll often send them $50 or $100 via Venmo or another cash app just to say thank you. It always means so much to them. The goal isn't to repay people for every favor they do, but no relationship should be one-sided, either. If someone does something nice for you, find creative ways to express your gratitude.

4. Don't Interrupt: Listen

"Not interrupting" and "listening" are two sides of the same coin, especially for leaders. Why? Because leadership often naturally requires that the leader speak and lead from the front, so we get used to hearing our voice first, most, and loudest. We can get in the habit of overriding and overruling other voices rather than taking the time to genuinely listen. But just because your role requires public speaking doesn't mean you are the only voice that should be heard, that your opinion is always right, or that you are the smartest person in the room.

Listening is not only good manners, it is a wise and effective leadership tactic.

109

First, because you learn new things when you let others speak; and second, because people's ownership in the team and the vision grows when they have a voice.

In your team meetings, learn how to ask excellent questions—and then stop talking. Let people answer without judging them, shutting them down, or excitedly running away with their answer. Let people interact with each other, even if the conversation gets a little heated or off topic. Ask "what if" questions to get people dreaming: *What if we opened a new location in that city? What if we hired this person? What if we tried to solve that problem? What if our product could do this? What if we tried to help people who have that need?* Get people imagining, interacting, and brainstorming, and then sit back and listen to what they come up with.

You are the leader, so you will need to interject comments or questions to guide the conversation from time to time, and you'll probably want to wrap up the discussion when it is over. But don't be in a hurry to make your ideas heard. Your attentive silence is an effective leadership tool, and it is one that communicates trust and value to your team.

ooo

Manners don't just make a man or woman—they make a leader, they make a team, and they make an organization. You will never outgrow the need to treat people with courtesy and respect. And as your influence grows, so will your need for good manners. Every interaction is important, and the casual, unplanned moments with people you encounter throughout the day are golden opportunities to build connections. A habit of good manners goes a long way toward building people skills and building people.

KEY TAKEAWAY

Develop a habit of treating people with courtesy and respect in every interaction, because your manners communicate who you are and how much you value others.

THIRTEEN

Reading Rooms, Reading People

I f you've ever attended a concert with a full orchestra, you probably remember the seconds of absolute silence before the music began, followed by the instant when the conductor, baton in hand, motioned to the orchestra and began the piece. It is a powerful, moving transition from silence to sound—one person leading dozens of musicians in a synchronized, captivating performance. There is actually an art to choosing the moment of transition, according to top conductor Leonard Bernstein (1919–1990).

Bernstein was one of the first American orchestra conductors to receive worldwide acclaim. Among the many things he is known for is composing the music for the musicals *West Side Story*, *Peter Pan*, and *Candide*. In addition to being a conductor, composer, author, music lecturer, pianist, and musical genius in general, he was an accomplished writer who shared his love and knowledge of music with others through his books. He had this to say about leading an orchestra:

> How can I describe to you the magic of the moment of beginning a piece of music? There is only one possible fraction of a second that feels exactly right for starting. There is a wait while the orchestra readies itself and collects its powers; while the conductor concentrates his whole will and force toward the work in hand; while the audience quiets down, and the last cough has died away. There is no slight rustle of a program book; the instruments are poised and— bang! That's it. One second later, it is too late, and the magic has vanished.[1]

111

You don't have to be a musician to catch the importance of timing in Leonard Bernstein's description. What fascinates me the most, though, is how attuned he was to his orchestra and his audience; or put another way, to his followers and to the larger world. He knew that the people in the room mattered just as much as the music, and that his role was not only to direct the orchestra, but also to discern timing, to be sensitive to the environment in which the music would be played.

Leaders need a similar attunement and sensitivity to those they lead and to their environment. We can't force our ideas on people or situations. We have to be able to read the environment and respond appropriately. We have to be in tune with where our followers are and where the world at large is at in any given moment. It's not enough to have the right ideas, we have to cultivate the art of knowing how best to present them, when to present them, and how to execute them. It's about coordinating a team and elevating their work for the watching world. And all of that requires developing a Bernstein-like sensitivity to reading the room and reading people.

Take Your Time

Reading, as I am using the term, refers to being aware of the state of a person or a roomful of people. That includes their emotions, their expectations, their needs, their desires, their goals, and more. "Reading a person" refers to one individual, and "reading a room" refers to a group of people, but both mean taking the time to understand the environment you are in before you get down to business.

Leaders can sometimes make the mistake of assuming their audience is in the same frame of mind they are, and they launch into whatever they planned to say with no regard for the emotional and mental state of those listening. It's not that they are wrong in what they say, but if people aren't ready to receive it, the message won't accomplish its goal.

You really can't execute a strategy in any meeting or conversation until you read the room and read the people. You can have a plan, you can have a goal, but your strategy should adjust if necessary when you actually walk into that auditorium, sit in that board meeting, or begin to negotiate that

112

deal. Why? Because there is always a human component, and that component is unpredictable. It's a cocktail of people's emotions, needs, fears, experiences, and personalities.

When you are in any business or social setting, take a moment to read the situation around you. Don't walk in with just your agenda, and don't assume everyone is on the same page as you. If you don't understand where people are, you'll never be able to serve them, and you'll never win with them. A little wisdom and patience in communication go a long way toward accomplishing leadership goals, whereas a lack of situational awareness can ruin opportunities, leave poor first impressions, and even hurt people around you.

Reading people includes emotional intelligence, as we discussed earlier, but it goes beyond that. It's about empathy, wisdom, and patience. Your goal, after all, is to serve people—so do your best to understand the people you are dealing with before trying to change, lead, or motivate them.

Maybe it's a *business deal* you'd love to close, but the other person isn't ready to make a decision. Just wait. Just listen. A *maybe* is better than a *no*, and you're more likely to get a no if you force a premature decision.

Maybe it's a *person* you would love to meet, but the setting is too rushed or chaotic. Don't force it. You'll likely have a chance to meet the person on another occasion; when you do, you'll be glad you didn't come across as desperate or inconsiderate.

Maybe it's a *decision* that needs to be made, but there are too many distractions for your team to think clearly, or you don't have the information you need, or something bigger is going on in the world right now and your decision needs to be postponed. Rushed decisions are rarely right decisions. Slow it down and wait until you can properly evaluate the next step.

Maybe it's a *correction or confrontation* that needs to take place, but the person isn't in a good place emotionally, or maybe you aren't in a healthy place at the moment yourself. Do both of you a favor and wait for the opportune moment. Set the conversation up for a win. Particularly if it's an issue that has been developing for months, you can probably wait a few more days to address it.

Maybe it's an exciting new *idea* you'd like to present but the team just got done successfully carrying out your last awesome, but slightly crazy,

113

idea, and they are exhausted. Read the room. Realize they need to celebrate, relax, and recoup. Your job is to see the future, but that doesn't mean you have to make the future happen now. Give people a little time off and then tackle the next awesome and crazy idea.

Reading people and rooms will help you do two things: determine the right *timing* and determine the right *approach*. Both are important, and learning how to assess them and then adjust on the fly will increase your effectiveness as a leader.

Timing refers to when you bring up a topic, push for a deal, or tackle a problem. "Timing is everything," says the popular phrase. Why? Because the right idea at the wrong time is, for all practical purposes, the wrong idea.

Every spouse has learned the hard way that there is a right time and a wrong time to bring up certain things. Ten o'clock at night after a long week is probably the worst time to tell your significant other about his or her annoying habit that frustrates you, for example. The same goes for any context in which you have influence or leadership. Take stock of the environment around you and wait for the right moment.

> Choosing the best approach is a practical expression of empathy.

Approach refers to the way you present a topic. Once you've figured out the best time to bring it up, decide how best to introduce it. This isn't manipulation, and it's not "spinning" things to your favor. It's simply meeting people where they are. It means showing them why they should care about what you are saying and how it helps, serves, or solves a problem. Choosing the best approach is a practical expression of empathy because in order to present something in a way that meets people's needs, you have to put yourself in their shoes.

Developing Your Reading Skills

Whether you are dealing with a person, a small group, or an auditorium full of listeners, your timing and approach will depend on the specific situation you encounter. You'll need to take into account all the factors and variables you possibly can, and it can be helpful to put yourself in the shoes of those you are leading or addressing. This is more art than science—that is, it is based more on intuition, experience, and skill than on a set of rules. However, there are several factors you should always notice when you enter a room or start a conversation, and these will take you a long way toward reading your audience.

1. Body Language

Reading body language is one of the most important keys to reading people and rooms because it plays a fundamental role in communicating emotions and attitudes. A classic study by Dr. Albert Mehabrian of the University of California Los Angeles found that only 7 percent of the emotional communication of a message is based on the words used. The rest—a whopping 93 percent—comes from vocal clues, such as tone of voice, volume, rate of speech, and vocal pitch (38 percent) and from facial expressions, hand gestures, and other forms of body language (55 percent). That doesn't mean you can know 93 percent of what people are *thinking* by their tone and body language, but you can probably pick up on a lot of what they are *feeling*—and sometimes that is what you most need to know. This is something we develop subconsciously as we grow and mature, but it is also a skill we can develop with practice.

Watch people and look for body language clues that might help you pick up on what they're feeling. Then speak not just to their minds, but to their hearts. Are they leaning in and engaged? Are their arms crossed defensively? Are they checking their phones in boredom? Can you hear stress, fear, insecurity, happiness, joy, or excitement in their voices? You can catch a lot by noticing people's posture, facial expressions, and tone.

2. Physical Needs

Pay attention to the time of day and how people are physically. Are they tired or hungry? Are they well-rested? Are they comfortable? Do they feel threatened? Do they need to stand up and stretch before continuing the meeting? Is it lunchtime? Is it the end of a long workday or workweek? According to Abraham Maslow's hierarchy of needs, our most basic human needs are physical. That means that until those physical needs are met, it's hard for us to focus on anything else. Think back to a time when you had to sit through an interminable meeting while needing to use the restroom and you'll know how quickly agenda items take a backseat to physical needs.

3. Distraction or Boredom

If you've ever addressed a roomful of junior high students (or even one junior high student, for that matter), you know the challenge of trying to communicate with someone who has a short attention span. Your options are to fight it or to work with it. It's been my experience that fighting it is a lose-lose situation, so I recommend working with it. Your goal is to serve people where they are, not make them conform to your expectations or personality type. You're the leader, so you can add more breaks, crack more jokes, or find ways to be more dynamic.

It's also important to know how to handle unexpected distractions. These can work in your favor if you don't let them throw you off. Sometimes a loud sneeze from somewhere down the hallway or a spilled cup of coffee is a great opportunity to give people a chance to laugh, relax, and take a brain break. People will take their cues from you, though. If you are irritated, people will get nervous or defensive, but if you see the humor in the situation and make a joke about it, you'll diffuse tension and bring people together. Plus, when you show people that you don't take yourself too seriously, you gain respect.

4. Emotional Distress

Family emergencies, economic needs, or other sources of worry can dramatically impact how individuals act. Part of reading people is learning to recognize when someone is dealing with something in their private life and it's spilling over into their work. Don't take their distraction personally, and don't just charge ahead with your agenda. Remember, life is bigger than your goals or business or idea. The person in front of you is the most important thing right now. He or she will likely be on your team long after your agenda item is old news, so set it aside and focus on being compassionate now.

5. External Events

The phrase "tone deaf" is often used to describe people who speak their mind with no regard for the cultural or social environment of the day, or without acknowledging a current natural disaster, crisis, or other news event that should take precedence. This often happens inadvertently when a company's scheduled social media post, which happens to be flippant or playful, hits right as a world tragedy is unfolding on international news. Similarly, leaders can seem tone deaf when they are so focused on the idea or the problem they're facing that they are insensitive to or oblivious of larger events. People live in the real world, not your world, so be aware of the events and concerns that matter to them.

While you can't know everything about what people are thinking or feeling, it's surprising how many clues you can decipher just by taking a few moments to pay attention and put yourself in other people's worlds.

These five factors—body language, physical needs, distraction or boredom, emotional distress, and external events—are the main things that can help inform your timing and approach.

ooo

The benefits of reading people and rooms are well worth the time and effort you put into them: better rapport with your listeners, more targeted communication, and better reception of your message. Whether you are conducting an orchestra like Leonard Bernstein, leading a staff meeting, or giving a keynote address, learning to read people and read the room is a key component to winning with people and succeeding as a leader.

KEY TAKEAWAY

Take time to become aware of where people are, both individually and as a group, before deciding how and when to communicate what is on your heart.

FOURTEEN

Become Their Biggest Cheerleader

W hat do you do when you are too discouraged or too tired to keep a positive mental attitude? As a lifelong basketball player, I can tell you exactly what I do: I listen to the cheerleaders around me. These are figurative cheerleaders, of course, but I learned this in high school when the cheerleaders were literal cheerleaders. And even though I knew it was their job to cheer me on, it still felt great to hear my name yelled from the sidelines or to draw on their energy when facing down a difficult opponent. They weren't my only cheerleaders, though. My mom, for example, was unfailingly supportive, and my coaches (when they weren't chewing me out) cheered me on as well.

High school sports are a microcosm of life, and just as athletes need cheerleaders to root them on, people within your sphere of influence need your encouragement and support. As a leader, make a commitment to be their biggest cheerleader. Their tasks can be challenging, progress can feel slow, and feelings of inadequacy, discouragement, and fatigue can set in. Your encouraging voice will help lift their spirits and renew their resolve.

Believe in Their Greatness

Most people need cheerleaders—those who believe in their greatness—because most people struggle with self-doubt. (And that goes for leaders too, if we're honest.) People often wonder if they really are great, if they have potential, if they are able to accomplish their goals. These feelings of self-doubt aren't necessarily a sign of weakness. A reasonable measure of doubt could mean people have a realistic view of themselves and that they take seriously the challenge they're facing. They don't want to overcommit, and they don't want to let people down. These are valid concerns and should be appreciated as such.

Sometimes, though, self-doubt goes too far and becomes an obstacle to what people are actually capable of achieving. Part of a leader's task is to call out the greatness within people, a greatness that might be buried beneath insecurity or fear. A leader peers around the doubts people harbor or hide behind in order to determine whether they are up to a particular challenge. And if they are, the leader works with them to overcome their doubts and help them believe in their own greatness.

Be the kind of leader who sees the greatness in people and speaks it into existence.

That means encouraging them in their potential even when they don't see it, and it means declaring what they can do even before they prove themselves. Faith comes before seeing, after all, and believing comes before tangible results. Leaders have faith in people, a faith that overcomes doubt.

And be careful not to define greatness too narrowly. Greatness comes in many forms. Greatness is more about faithfulness than fame. It's about fulfilling potential, about achieving dreams, and about influencing others for good. Greatness is becoming the best version of yourself. That could mean being a stay-at-home parent and raising children. It could mean running a successful business. It could mean going back to school and starting a new career. It could mean launching a nonprofit dedicated to helping people. Greatness lies within everyone, and leaders are uniquely positioned to recognize and encourage it in their people, and then to help them navigate any obstacles along the way.

Every human being has the potential for greatness. Ask children what they want to be when they grow up, and their dreams are usually hero-level dreams, unfettered by thoughts of failure or obstacles and often focused on helping people: firefighter, police officer, astronaut, doctor, veterinarian. Their future is going to be great; they are sure of it. As time goes on and "real life" sinks in, though, those kids became adults with school debt and mortgages and kids of their own. Often, they begin to give up on greatness and settle for survival. Their expectations sink, their self-efficacy suffers, and their lives are characterized more by risk management than risk taking.

Your role as leader is not to create greatness in people, but to restore their belief in their own greatness. You can't make them be great, but you can help them overcome the obstacles and the mental blocks that get in the way of their potential. You can encourage them to learn, grow, try again, forgive, believe, and win. Shakespeare wrote,

> Our doubts are traitors,
> and make us lose the good we oft might win,
> by fearing to attempt.[1]

Be the voice that helps people overcome their fears and accomplish their dreams. When they are facing a tough opponent, let them know that you are cheering them on, that you believe in them even when they doubt themselves. Most people are starved for encouragement because they get so little of it. And yet, encouragement is the easiest thing to give people: all it takes is a decision to be a cheerleader and a little discernment to discover their unique potential for greatness.

Build Their Confidence

Becoming your team's greatest cheerleader starts with believing in their greatness and encouraging them to believe it as well. But how exactly can you convince people that they are capable of great things, especially when they may have spent most of their lives believing the opposite?

We looked earlier at the importance of self-talk and self-confidence, and I mentioned the work of psychologist Albert Bandura and his theory of self-efficacy, which refers to how confident people are in their own abilities. Part of Bandura's research focused on what he called *verbal persuasion* or *social persuasion.* Unlike self-talk, verbal persuasion refers to the fact that what *others* think and say about your abilities has the power to shape what *you* think about your abilities. Bandura believed that verbal persuasion was among the key factors in developing self-efficacy. He writes:

> People who are persuaded verbally that they possess the capabilities to master given activities are likely to mobilize greater effort and sustain it than if they harbor self-doubts and dwell on personal deficiencies when problems arise.[2]

Since then, countless studies have applied Bandura's ideas to everything from junior high academics to college success and career choices, all with consistent results: there is a direct link between the verbal encouragement people receive and their subsequent confidence and performance levels.

This has significant implications for leaders. When you believe in others and encourage them, you shape their self-view, build their confidence, and contribute to their success. Conversely, if you express disbelief in their abilities, or if you continually point out their flaws and deficiencies, you can actually weaken their confidence and hinder their advancement. That's why negativity is rarely, if ever, a good motivational strategy. To put it another way, you can encourage people into their destiny, but you can't shame them into it.

What does verbal encouragement look like? First of all, *verbal encouragement should be sincere.* You have to believe what you are saying. If you can't say something sincerely encouraging to someone, you might need to either reevaluate your attitude or reevaluate the person's role, because leaders have to believe in the people on their team.

Second, *verbal encouragement should be specific.* This requires a little work. One-size-fits-all compliments and clichés might be easier, but they mean less. Instead of "you're the best," or "you're so amazing," you might say, "I am in awe of your organizational abilities" or "I loved how you handled that customer's complaint."

Finally, *verbal encouragement should be frequent.* Self-confidence leaks, and people need to be filled up regularly. Cheerleaders never stop cheering: they shout encouragement throughout the game, whether or not the team is winning and whether or not players seem to need it. Likewise, leaders should continually focus on building the confidence of their team members.

In addition to verbal encouragement, Bandura's research identified another important factor that contributes to self-efficacy, something he calls *mastery experiences*. The term, as he defines it, refers to personal experiences of success. In other words, if you've had a measure of success already, you will be more likely to believe you'll continue to succeed. "Successes build a robust belief in one's personal efficacy," he writes.[3]

Good leaders use both of these things—verbal encouragement and mastery experiences—to build confidence in others. Bandura continues:

> Successful efficacy builders do more than convey positive appraisals. In addition to raising people's beliefs in their capabilities, they structure situations for them in ways that bring success and avoid placing people in situations prematurely where they are likely to fail often. They measure success in terms of self-improvement rather than by triumphs over others.[4]

That means that leaders look for ways to set people up for success. Good leaders are not just cheerleaders; they are *realistic* cheerleaders. Don't lie to people about what they can do: that only leads to disappointment when they try and fail. You need to know them and to believe in them, to see the best in them and to draw that out. That means encouraging them to try, and it also means giving them appropriate opportunities for mastery experiences and actively supporting their progress and improvement.

How do you create mastery experiences for people? How do you set them up for success? Before I answer that, think for a moment about how babies learn to walk. My wife and I have lived through this stage multiple times, and it's both exhilarating and terrifying.

When toddlers are taking their first steps, parents do everything in their power to set them up for success (and to avoid trips to the ER). First, they clear a path, moving coffee tables, lamps, vases, and anything else that might break or cause injury. They start with very short distances, because toddlers don't really walk at first—they fall with style, to paraphrase an iconic *Toy Story* line. Parents stand close to the child, hands extended, ready to cushion potential falls. And with every step, every new stage, they cheer and celebrate as if the toddler just finished a marathon.

Now, let's apply that to leadership. First, as much as possible, *foresee obstacles*. Think ahead to potential roadblocks and help people avoid or navigate those. They may not know the problems they could run into, but you likely do; rather than letting those obstacles potentially discourage people, help them plan ahead. Give them tools, strategies, or resources to avoid things that could hinder their success.

Second, *start with small goals*. Don't give someone fresh out of college your biggest account. Don't put a junior designer in charge of branding a national advertising campaign. Don't have someone who has never spoken more than five minutes in public give a keynote presentation. Start small, let people taste success, and then give them incrementally bigger challenges.

> People have greatness within them, but they often need someone who consistently believes in them in order to fulfill their potential.

Third, *stay close by*. Or to put it another way, leave room for failure. They probably won't be totally successful on the first try. Be available to help them rather than standing at a distance, watching them fail spectacularly. Just as toddlers do, your team members are likely to pick up a few bumps and bruises along the way, and they'll learn from those as well. But do your best to minimize the pain and maximize the joy of the growing process.

Finally, *celebrate every stage*. Growth and progress are important and deserve to be recognized. Every stage is a mini victory, a small mastery experience, on the way to ever-greater triumphs.

The personal successes of the people you lead become planks in a platform of self-confidence. They provide a place to stand, a solid position from which to face the challenges of life. When you give verbal encouragement and create mastery experiences for your team, you replace their doubt in themselves with confidence in their potential, and you set them up for even more audacious goals.

ooo

If you want to win with people, become their biggest fan, their loudest cheerleader, their most committed supporter.

Over the years, I've seen time and time again that loyalty is a two-way street, and so is believing in people. The more you believe in others, the more they'll believe in you. People will open their hearts to someone who has confidence in their potential and their greatness, and they will follow a leader who cheers for them.

KEY TAKEAWAY

Be people's biggest cheerleader by believing in them and helping them believe in themselves.

FIFTEEN

The Most Important Currency

n January 2014, thirty-year-old Gerald Cotten, owner of Canada's largest cryptocurrency company, QuadrigaCX, died suddenly while on his honeymoon in India. In his sole possession were the passwords to access all of his users' funds, a total of approximately $190 million Canadian dollars ($145 million US). His colleagues initially reported that the funds were inaccessible due to the missing login information. *Business Insider* pretty much summed up the situation with its headline, "A crypto exchange can't repay $190 million it owes customers because its CEO died with the only password."[1]

The story didn't end there, though. A few weeks later, a court-appointed auditor obtained Cotten's laptop and other devices and determined that the digital wallets that supposedly contained millions in bitcoin had been quietly emptied eight months before Cotten's death. It also discovered that QuadrigaCX didn't have a basic accounting system in place, and that Mr. Cotten had sole and total access to all monies invested. At the end of the audit, investors were left with no funds, no answers, and no easy path to pursue repayment.

Like many cases of financial mismanagement and fraud, we may never know the full story of what happened or where the money went. But if you're like me, you're probably wondering how $145 million can be stashed—and lost—from "digital wallets." But my point with this story isn't that we should avoid cryptocurrency; it's that even an invisible currency can have great value. Bitcoin and other cryptocurrencies may be intangible and hard to understand, but there is no denying they have a very tangible value and a direct, wide-ranging effect.

The same could be said of another invisible "currency" that all of us have access to. This currency is not stored in digital wallets or tracked on Wall Street, and it would be difficult to put a monetary value on it, yet it has a profound and far-reaching effect on our success in just about every area of life. It's the currency of *relationship*.

Relational Equity

The concept that relationships have a value is sometimes referred to as *relational equity*. Mohanbir Sawhney, a professor at Northwestern University and a noted management consultant, defines relational equity in the corporate context as "the wealth-creating potential that resides in the firm's relationships with its stakeholders."[2] In other words, the connections we have with people are assets, just like cash on hand, stock, inventory, real estate, or other tangible property. They might not be listed on our balance sheet, but they are assets nonetheless.

Sawhney continues, "Competitive advantage no longer stems first and foremost from the firm's ownership of physical assets, as has generally been the case since the dawn of the Industrial Revolution, but rather from its ability to build and leverage relationships with customers, partners, suppliers, and employees."[3] His point is that relationships are worth investing in, cultivating, and protecting. Relational equity may not be easily quantifiable, but that doesn't make it any less real than dollars or yen or bitcoin.

I think most leaders intuitively know that relationships can be valuable assets. Whether we are leading in the world of business, entertainment, church, education, sports, or just about anything else, *who we know* can open doors and create opportunities. So it makes good business sense to "build and leverage relationships," as Sawhney puts it. But even though we believe relationships matter, we can get so focused on the bottom line, on growth, or on systems and strategies that we forget to make relationships one of our top priorities.

I'm not saying we should invest in people just so we can get something from them later. When Sawhney says we should "leverage relationships," he doesn't use leverage in a manipulative sense but rather a practical one: you need to know whom you can count on and whom to turn to in times of need.

If you sincerely invest in people, value them, serve them, and cultivate a genuine connection with them, you will receive a return on your investment.

While your main relationships (outside of family and friends, of course) will be with people directly related to your area of work or service, such as employees, clients, customers, donors, church members, and providers, keep in mind that *all* people matter, not just those who directly contribute to your goals. You can and should build connections with people wherever possible, even when they aren't directly participating in your endeavor or vision.

I've heard the opposite from time to time, by the way. I've seen some people, especially on social media, who advocate cutting out of your life anyone who isn't helping you reach your goals. That makes me a little uncomfortable for two reasons. First, it would make your world revolve around you and your goals, which is—no offense—a small world. Second, you never know who, when, or how someone will actually help you with your goals. I suspect the people who advocate cutting people out are mostly trying to avoid distractions or unhealthy criticism, and there is a place for that. We looked earlier at the importance of listening to the right voices. But don't be too quick to cut people out of your life just because they aren't serving your immediate purposes. They are people, and therefore they have value. To the extent you are able, strive to honor them, love them, and add value to them.

Deposits and Withdrawals

We know intuitively that relationships matter, as I said earlier, but how do we build them? How do we add value and build trust? How do we invest in people in such a way that our connection with them grows? Relationships don't just happen. They take intentionality, work, and time. If we understand how to build relationships properly, they will withstand the ups and downs of life and the inevitable bumps in the road.

One way to think about building relationships is in terms of *deposits* and *withdrawals*. Not in the sense of reducing friendship and affection to a mere transaction, of course, but in the sense of investment. The more we put into a relationship, the more it will thrive, grow, and generate a return. But if all we do is take or withdraw from a relationship, the balance will quickly drop to zero and it will cease to be an asset we can count on.

Every leader needs to understand how to make deposits and withdrawals in the relational sphere. People keep a record, whether intentionally or not, of how you treat them; and you have a balance, whether you know it or not, that is either positive or negative. As a leader, part of learning to win with people is becoming aware of that relational balance and managing it well.

You build your relational balance when you make deposits, such as showing love, giving praise, serving, expressing loyalty, and spending time together. Relational deposits build loyalty, longevity, trust. That positive balance is what allows you to make withdrawals when needed. A withdrawal is anything that could "take" from the relationship, such as a request, a confrontation, a misunderstanding, a change, a difficult decision, or an absence.

Both deposits and withdrawals are part of any normal relationship. You won't always be able to be a patient, wise, perfect leader—not by a long shot! But if you are intentional about building a positive balance with people, about strengthening your relationship through regular deposits, then the occasional withdrawal won't "overdraw your account."

My goal with my team, my employees, and even my family and friends is to always keep a positive balance. I try to be aware of where I stand with people in every sphere of my life. I don't want to be in relational debt to anyone: I don't want to feel guilty when I think about them, hide when I see them, or never be able to ask them another favor because I've used too many already. Below is a list of practical things I do to make relational deposits. You'll notice many of them are simply good people skills and good manners, which we've discussed already.

- Remember names
- Speak encouraging words (be a cheerleader)
- Express gratitude often, especially in public
- Remember birthdays and celebrate them somehow, even if it's just a hug or a shout-out
- Be present when they speak; listen attentively
- Text or call, and return texts and calls
- Send gift cards, flowers, or other small gifts
- Give hugs, high fives, a pat on the back, or other appropriate expressions of physical affection
- Fulfill commitments on time
- Help out with projects
- Eat, laugh, and have fun together

Learn what means the most and speaks the loudest to people and focus on those things. Conversely, avoid letting them down in areas you know are important to them. As in everything, this is about serving people best.

Building relational equity is primarily about thoughtfulness and about identifying what best serves the other person.

Author Gary Chapman's perennially bestselling book *The Five Love Languages* states that each of us has a primary and a secondary love language, or way of showing and perceiving love. He identifies five specific languages: gifts, quality time, words of affirmation, acts of service, and physical touch. His premise is that if someone attempts to show their affection to you using a different language than yours, you won't feel as loved, and if they fail you in an area related to your primary love language, it will hurt you more deeply than it would if it were a different type of failure. Married couples, for example, often have different love languages, so they can end up hurting each other inadvertently simply because they don't realize how deeply their actions and words affect one another. Chapman encourages his readers to identify their own language and those of their spouse, children, and others in their lives in order to better communicate love and to avoid misunderstanding.

Building a positive relational balance comes down to being aware of where you stand with people and taking that into account in your interactions with them. Put yourself in their shoes. Keep track of how well you've done at meeting expectations and commitments to them. You can only show up late to so many meetings before followers lose respect or your boss lets you go. You can only forget to text a friend back so many times before you come across as disinterested or rude. You can only stay late at the office so many nights before your family stops appreciating your hard work and begins to resent it. Whether you are a boss, spouse, parent, teacher, pastor, or other leader, simply being aware of the status of the relationship will help you navigate it better.

Keeping a Positive Balance

Leaders can't meet every need and every expectation, which means we will fail people or let them down from time to time. We will also have to engage in a certain amount of correction, which is not necessarily pleasant, and a certain amount of "making" people do things that are part of their job, which isn't fun either. Put all those things together and leaders have the potential to make a lot of relational withdrawals.

That means we need to be even more intentional about offsetting the inevitable withdrawals in order to maintain a healthy balance. On one hand, we can't make every decision to meet people's expectations or to guard their feelings. But on the other hand, we can't discount the negative effect of those difficult leadership moments. So how do we keep a positive balance?

The first thing is to *focus on making proactive deposits*. In other words, make deposits whenever, wherever, and however you can, knowing that withdrawals will happen at some point. Regular relational deposits build a balance that permits occasional withdrawals without going into relational deficit. On the other hand, if there is a zero balance or negative balance, each withdrawal will feel far more negative because you are incurring an even greater relational debt.

To illustrate, imagine you have an employee you don't know well. Maybe she works in another part of the building or is a couple of rungs down the organizational ladder. One day she makes a big mistake, and you realize you need to talk to her about it. You show up at her desk, explain the issue clearly (maybe even forcefully), accept her apology and her promise to change, and then leave. Was that a successful encounter? I'd argue that it probably wasn't, or at least it was far from ideal. Not because you said something wrong or overstepped your boundaries (you're the leader, so presumably you didn't) or because she reacted wrongly (she didn't either), but simply because you now have a clear negative balance with her. Her only significant interaction with you in her entire career consisted of you getting on her case for a mistake—and that's not a good feeling for anyone. However, if you had already built up a positive relational balance with her—by complimenting her work or expressing gratitude for her role—the correction would have had far less emotional impact because it would have occurred in the context of a trusting relationship.

I'm not saying you have to butter someone up before you tell them where they've failed, or that you can't ever confront someone you don't know well. I'm just saying that the ideal approach is to be proactive about building a relational balance and developing trust, because you never know when you'll need it.

Relational withdrawals happen for many reasons, not just correction. But the same positive balance, built by the same thoughtful words and actions, will help protect the relationship from the painful or difficult moments that come along.

The second key to keeping a positive relational balance is to *apologize when you've failed*. Apologies go a long way toward restoring balance. Unlike debts measured in dollars and cents—which are rarely forgiven—people usually welcome apologies and are quick to forgive. If they aren't, it's possible that something deeper is going on or that your offense is more serious than one or two failures. In a healthy relationship, both parties want things to work. That means the offended person is probably hoping you will want to make things right, too, and will respond well when you acknowledge the situation humbly.

Forgiveness is a powerful tool, and it works both ways. When you grant forgiveness to others for mistakes they've made, or when you request forgiveness for mistakes you've made, you help offset the negative effects of the error. Don't wait for the other person to take the initiative, regardless of who is at fault—just seek reconciliation. Usually, both people are partly to blame anyway, so take responsibility for what you can, ask forgiveness as needed, and work toward a resolution.

If you have made a withdrawal for a necessary correction or confrontation, don't apologize—you didn't do anything wrong. As a leader, you have to have the freedom to lead, and that includes having difficult conversations and making difficult decisions. However, you can make sure the person didn't take it too personally, you can thank them for responding well and keeping a good attitude, and you can find ways to give affirmation in other areas. In other words, even when you don't need to apologize, you should still look for ways to offset the negative impacts of withdrawals.

The third way to keep a positive relational balance is to *be intentional about paying off debt*. Of course, if you had enough equity going into the blunder or confrontation or whatever withdrawal has happened, there may not be any debt; but even the strongest relationships can be rocked by offense, error, insults, misunderstandings, and conflict from time to time. As leaders, we must be aware when we have let someone down and seek to make it up to them.

Unfortunately, it often takes multiple deposits to offset one big withdrawal. If you've ever forgotten your spouse's birthday, you know how hard it is to dig yourself out of certain holes. That's because humans tend to feel negative emotions more easily and intensely than positive ones. In economics, this is referred to as *loss aversion*: people would rather avoid loss than acquire equivalent gains. Some studies have suggested that losses are felt twice as much, psychologically, as gains.[4] That means if you have to challenge or correct someone, or you forget a birthday, or you show up late to an important meeting, or you snap at someone, or you have any other perceived failure or offense, people are likely to feel it more deeply than a comparable act of goodness. I realize that's not terribly encouraging, but it's reality.

Again, apologies and forgiveness work wonders. That's the first step, but don't stop there. Look for ways to restore, to repay, to make things right again. That might take a little effort, but it's usually not as hard and it doesn't take as long as you might think. People tend to be quick to forgive leaders who truly want to do right by them.

Those three things—regular deposits, quick apologies, and making things right—will go a long way toward keeping your relational accounts in good health. Over time, those relationships will become your most treasured asset of all.

ooo

Just like bitcoin, the invisible currency of relationships has real and tangible value. But unlike bitcoin, relationships aren't stored in digital wallets or locked behind passwords: they are in our hearts; they are seated around our boardroom tables; they are accessible by email or texting or phone calls. Some of them are living in our homes. People matter, therefore relationships matter, and they are worth investing in at every opportunity.

KEY TAKEAWAY

Invest in your most valuable asset—relationships—by intentionally and continually making deposits into other people.

SIXTEEN

Narcissism Never Wins

In Greek mythology, Narcissus was a young hunter renowned for his beauty—and for spurning any suitor who pursued him. One day while he was in the woods, the nymph Echo saw him and immediately fell in love. She caught his attention, but he rejected her. Heartbroken, Echo wandered the forest, pining over the unrequited love to the point that she faded away, leaving behind only the sound of her voice. When the goddess Nemesis heard about the incident, she decided to punish Narcissus. She led him to a spring, where he caught sight of his own reflection and promptly fell in love . . . with himself. He remained there, staring into the water—enthralled by his own beauty but unable to be loved back by his reflection—until he wasted away and died.

This two-thousand-year-old story is where we get the modern term *narcissism*, which is frequently used in popular culture as a synonym for selfishness and self-centeredness. A narcissistic person is self-absorbed and self-important. In a word, selfish.

Narcissism to the extreme is a clinical condition called *narcissistic personality disorder*. The American Psychiatric Association defines it as "a pattern of need for admiration and lack of empathy for others. A person with narcissistic personality disorder may have a grandiose sense of self-importance, a sense of entitlement, take advantage of others or lack empathy."[1] The Mayo Clinic calls it "a mental condition in which people have an inflated sense of their own importance, a deep need for excessive attention and admiration, troubled relationships, and a lack of empathy for others." Interestingly they add, "But behind this mask of extreme confidence lies a fragile self-esteem that's vulnerable to the slightest criticism."[2]

In most people, of course, narcissism does not reach the level of a full-blown personality disorder. But tendencies toward selfishness, ego, self-absorption, an excessive need for admiration, and a lack of empathy are all too common in society and in leadership today; and in that sense, narcissism is alive and well. As leaders, we must be aware of these tendencies both in ourselves and in the cultures we build in our teams and organizations.

Beyond Selfishness

Humans are born with a selfish bent—any parent can tell you that. The first words of a child after *Mama* and *Dada* are usually *no* and *mine,* accompanied by screaming. A key task of parenting is helping children realize they are not a universe unto themselves, but members of a family and part of a larger world. Good manners, sharing with others, empathy, deference, conflict resolution—these things should be taught first in the home, with the goal of preparing children for the world that awaits. It's a world where, contrary to popular opinion, selfishness actually doesn't do well. We teach children social skills and character traits because we know they will need these things to have friends, to hold down jobs, to contribute to society, and to lead others.

Humans are meant to grow beyond selfishness, not to internalize and institutionalize it. Maturity is seeing beyond the immediate, beyond the bubble that is your world. It is realizing that your life is intricately connected with others. Their success is your success, and their pain is your pain, because no one lives alone. John Donne's famous seventeenth-century essay "No Man Is an Island" says this:

> No man is an island entire of itself; every man
> is a piece of the continent, a part of the main;
> if a clod be washed away by the sea, Europe

is the less, as well as if a promontory were, as
well as any manner of thy friends or of thine
own were; any man's death diminishes me,
because I am involved in mankind.
And therefore never send to know for whom
the bell tolls; it tolls for thee.[3]

It is also to inspire others to serve and give—to step into relationship
and teamwork. You can't help others grow if you are stuck in selfishness,
though, and until you can get over your-
self, you'll never serve others. Rejecting
narcissism and embracing selflessness
and generosity are constant challenges
for any leader.

> As a leader, your role is to serve and to give, which flies in the face of narcissism.

A greater title or a bigger sphere of
influence simply gives you more power
to serve. In other words, leadership greatness isn't in the power you have
over people but in the power with which you serve them.

If you serve people instead of using people, you'll always have great
people around you. People don't want to be used. They don't want to be
leveraged or manipulated. They want to be believed in and built up. Narcissistic leadership might appear to work short-term; even a self-absorbed
leader can threaten, bribe, and manipulate people into a certain amount
of productivity. But this kind of shallow, self-serving leadership won't win
long-term. If you want to succeed, serve people. Make your life about others, not about ego.

Seven Signs of a Narcissistic Leader

How can you identify narcissism in yourself as a leader? It's not easy. For
one thing, selfishness is a matter of degrees, not an either-or distinction.
It's normal and healthy to care for yourself, to look out for your interests,
and to be proud of yourself. But when those things take precedence, or
when they trump empathy and compassion, you've begun to cross a line.

Since human beings tend to give themselves the benefit of the doubt long after they should, you might think you have good motivations and a balanced perspective when really, you're spending too much time admiring your own reflection in the water.

The American Psychiatric Association's definition of *narcissism*, quoted above, gives us a picture of selfishness taken to an extreme. It highlights several characteristics of narcissism that are very applicable to leaders. To be clear, I'm not saying that if we have one of these characteristics, then we have a clinical personality disorder. But there is a possibility that we have allowed an internal bent toward selfishness and self-absorption to take root in our leadership, and it needs to be corrected before it grows further. That is healthy self-examination, and it is part of leading ourselves first. Here, then, are seven signs of a narcissistic leader.

1. Excessive Need for Admiration

Admiration feels good, but it's a monster that is never satiated. A self-absorbed leader cannot receive enough praise, credit, or glory to be satisfied. If you are relying on your team or your spouse to fill that void by singing your praises, you'll burn them out. Separate your value from your accomplishments and be secure even if no one is asking for your autograph. That way, when fame does come along, you'll be prepared to handle it properly.

2. Lack of Empathy

This may be the most dangerous consequence of narcissism. Selfish leaders tend to use people, ignore people, reject people, and step on people. It's not that they do it on purpose, but there is simply little room for understanding or compassion in their thought processes because their entire existence is focused on themselves. And since they are not really thinking about other people's feelings or needs, they end up hurting others. If you find yourself consistently treating people poorly, or if there is a growing trail of people behind you who have left your team in hurt or anger, evaluate your empathy level. Make sure you are thinking not just about yourself, but about others as well.

138

3. Exaggerated Sense of Self-Importance

You *are* important—you just shouldn't think about that all the time, and you should also remember that other people are equally as important as you. If you can manage to hold on to the dual truth that both you and those around you are important, you'll be able to have healthy self-confidence and self-esteem without falling into egotism. A healthy question to ask yourself is this: *What informs my sense of self-importance?* If the answer is something as transient as a job title, money, or fame, adjust the basis of your self-image before ego gets out of hand (or crashes and burns if things take a downturn later). Focus instead on things that are more permanent and more under your control: your relationships, moral strength, character growth, spirituality, and contribution to others.

4. Feelings of Entitlement

We've all been around people who thought the world owed them something, and it's not an attractive trait. Leaders, even good ones, can adopt this same attitude, often subtly and over time. Remember, you will make sacrifices that no one else makes. You will carry weight that no one else understands. If you don't process that reality correctly along the way, you can begin to resent the sacrifices—or worse, resent those you lead—and feel entitled to "extras." Corruption easily

Be wary if you find yourself consistently hosting pity parties in your head.

follows entitlement, because you can begin to feel above the law, as if the rules that apply to lesser mortals somehow don't apply to you.

That can be an indication that you're developing a victim mentality, which is often a precursor to feelings of entitlement and the temptations that follow.

5. Taking Advantage of Others

Narcissism blinds leaders to the needs, dreams, and rights of others, and it creates leaders who use people rather than serving people. If your thoughts are all about you, you will view others through a narcissistic lens: how they can serve you, how they can advance your goals, whether or not they are worth your time and investment. As a leader, you do have to maintain the integrity of your cause, but you can't burn through people in service of your cause. Even if someone moves on from your group, you can still value and honor the relationship. Also, don't make the mistake of limiting your attention and care just to the people who will help you reach your objectives. The way you treat people who aren't useful to you is a good litmus test of your character as a leader.

6. Broken or Limited Relationships

In their book *The Narcissism Epidemic: Living in the Age of Entitlement*, authors Jean Twenge and Keith Campbell state that narcissists tend to lack "emotionally warm, caring, and loving relationships with other people." They add, "This is a main difference between a narcissist and someone merely high in self-esteem: the high self-esteem person who's not narcissistic values relationships, but the narcissist does not."[4] In other words, self-centered, self-absorbed people tend to have poor relationships—but they don't even care because they don't value connection with others in the first place.

As leaders, our relationships serve as a barometer of our heart. They reveal how others-focused our thoughts and actions are. If we lack strong, vibrant connections with people, or if we routinely shut ourselves off from others, we may be drifting toward narcissistic patterns. On the other hand, strong, long-term relationships likely indicate that our ego is under control.

7. Overreaction to Criticism

Criticism is inevitable, especially when you are in leadership, and it can be hard to take it graciously. Temporary feelings of hurt, wounded pride, or defensiveness are probably normal. But if criticism triggers major negative reactions, you might have a problem with narcissism. These reactions could include lashing out in revenge at critics, making excuses or blaming other people for your mistakes, loudly and constantly proclaiming your innocence, falling into depression or experiencing prolonged moodiness, and so on.

Why does narcissism trigger an overreaction to criticism? In part, because an overinflated ego frequently hides deep insecurity. One of the more subtle truths about narcissism is that it often involves a sort of hidden self-rejection. You can become so consumed with fixing or hiding your faults that you can't think about anything else. Humorist and writer Emily Levine said it this way: "I am a recovering narcissist. I thought narcissism was about self-love till someone told me there is a flip side to it. It is actually drearier than self-love; it is unrequited self-love."[5] This is why it is so important for leaders to both accept themselves and lead themselves: if you can't move past your failures and shortcomings, you'll tend to overreact defensively to anyone who threatens your fragile ego.

ooo

Young Narcissus, staring at his reflection, would have made a terrible leader. He couldn't take his eyes off himself, so he couldn't leave the edge of the water. The same thing can happen if we take our eyes off the vision, off the challenges ahead, and—most important—off the people around us, and turn our gaze inward in narcissistic self-adoration. When we do that, we stop leading others and end up simply serving ourselves. That's the polar opposite of productive, visionary leadership.

Narcissism is inherently unsatisfactory, and in the long run, it never wins. What does win? Kindness wins. Altruism wins. Servant leadership wins. Celebrating other people wins. Success isn't measured by how many people know your name. It isn't even measured by what you accomplish in your lifetime. It's measured by your coaching tree, your mentoring chain. It's measured by the fruit you cultivate in other people's lives. It's measured by the investments you make in people that, twenty years later, are still earning compound interest. It's measured by what you give, not by what you receive; and by who you serve, not by who serves you.

KEY TAKEAWAY

Make sure your leadership is focused not on yourself, but on serving, building, and caring for others.

141

SEVENTEEN

Time Will Tell

Online dating is a unique world, as anyone who has tried it will tell you. It has benefits, challenges, dangers, and quirks that society is still learning to navigate. And it's more than a passing trend: a Stanford analysis of data from 2017 found that 39 percent of new couples that year met online and that "for heterosexual couples in the US, meeting online has become the most popular way couples meet."[1] Dating apps are an essential element of the online dating experience, which is why terms such as "swipe left" and "swipe right" have so quickly become part of mainstream culture. And that brings up two big questions that face online daters today: *How can someone possibly tell who I am just by looking at me? How can I tell if someone is a good match just by looking at their picture and profile?*

According to a survey quoted by the dating site eHarmony, 53 percent of online dating users have lied on their profile, providing false information about things such as height, weight, lifestyle, age, and income.[2] Clearly, scrolling through a lineup of photos and profiles has its limitations. We know that. We can't really tell just by looking at a picture and a description whether someone is reliable, smart, kind, responsible, honest, or mature. But we still try. It's surprising how fast our brains make judgments based on faces and first impressions, and how confident we are in those snap judgments.

Alexander Todorov, author of the book *Face Value: The Irresistible Influence of First Impressions*, conducted a study in which participants were asked to draw trait inferences from the facial appearance of other people. He wanted to discover just how fast people make up their minds about others, based solely on their faces. He studied five trait judgments—attractiveness, likeability, trustworthiness, competence, and aggressiveness. With every trait, he found that the judgments people made in 1/10 of a second were essentially the same as judgments made with no time constraints at all. In other words, they only took a fraction of a second to evaluate key moral and character issues.[3] That is amazing—and slightly terrifying if you are still in the dating scene.

In certain contexts, quick judgments such as these could be helpful. For example, if you're sizing up a new social situation and are trying to fit in, or if you find yourself in a threatening situation and need to know whom to trust. On the other hand, these lightning-fast subconscious decisions are also partly to blame for things such as racial profiling and ethnic stereotyping. To assume anything about someone's character or values based on the color of their hair or skin or language is inherently wrong.

There are many ways in which we form our impressions and judgments of people. They might be based on *things we observe or know* about people, such as their physical features, economic class, educational background, family background, nationality, or speaking abilities or habits. Or, they could come from *things we've heard about them* from others: past experiences, failures, successes, conflicts, flaws, or strengths. Finally, they might be determined by *our first encounters* with them, such as initial judgments about their intelligence, abilities, character, or potential. All of these things aren't necessarily wrong, but they aren't necessarily right, either.

It should be clear that while we do need to make some level of judgment based on first impressions (indeed, we couldn't stop doing it even if we tried), we must also recognize the inherently subjective and superficial nature of the process. And we should hold our opinions loosely, willing to change them as time reveals the truth about people. This is especially true, as we will see, in leadership.

Slow to Judge

We meet new people all the time. This includes possible new hires, customers and clients, potential investors, volunteers, and more. Evaluating people quickly, therefore, is sort of a necessary evil in leadership. It is both a skill to be developed and a liability to keep in check, a pressing need and a big risk. To accurately judge someone's character, trustworthiness, capabilities, and potential requires a big dose of humility and a willingness to continually reevaluate our judgments.

Pay attention to your snap judgments and manage them wisely. While you may not be able to disable your brain's facial scanning feature, you can choose to reserve final judgment on people until you know more about them. Ask them questions about themselves. Do a little digging to get a clearer picture, such as calling references. Allow your initial evaluation to be informed, modified, or completely replaced by actual data as time goes on. And along the way, until time proves you right or wrong, you can strive to give them the benefit of the doubt, believing the best rather than expecting the worst.

Snap judgments can be positive as well as negative, and you need to manage those too. Sometimes leaders hire or promote or partner with people too quickly. It's possible to have an overly optimistic view of people and to put them in roles for which they're either not a good fit or aren't yet ready. Whether your judgments are positive, negative, or somewhere between, be careful how much stock you place in your first impressions.

The people around you are far too complex to be reduced to a few split-second labels. Just as you want others to let you be you, without labeling you and filing you away in an arbitrary category in their brain, so you must give people time to surprise you. People often have hidden gifts—and hidden flaws—that only time will reveal. Leaders should be good judges of character and ability, but good judgment is often *slow* judgment. Take your time and build some history together.

History Is the Best Teacher

Snap judgments, as we have seen, have their limitations, but history is a far more accurate indicator of people's true character and capabilities. That is precisely the reason most jobs require a résumé. If you're sitting across the desk from someone you just met and are considering them for an important position, you want to know whom the person has worked for, what he or she did there, how long the job lasted, and—maybe most important—why the person left that role.

Outside of job applicants, though, you don't usually have the opportunity to review people's résumés when you first meet them. And yet, their history is still very important. As leaders, how can we allow people's history to inform our opinion of them? How can we leverage the revealing power of time to make the best decisions about whom to work with, whom to hire, whom to promote, whom to partner with, whom to buy from or sell to, whom to build with, whom to trust? Here are three practical ways to make history work for you.

1. Learn Their Backstory

Everyone has a backstory: a personal history, a past, a context. That backstory influences everything about them in subtle and sometimes unconscious ways. It affects who they are, how they react to correction, what they fear, how much risk they can handle, how they'll respond to your authority, how much they will trust you, and how they work with others. A backstory is not a good thing or a bad thing, it's just a thing—something to keep in mind in all your interactions, especially if they report directly to you in some work or volunteer capacity. Maybe they were mistreated by a former leader, and they see you in the same light. Maybe they grew up spoiled, and you're the first person to tell them no. Maybe they've failed a few times and are hesitant to try—and maybe fail—again.

Get as much context as you can about people, both before and after you bring them on your team, because you can't serve someone you don't understand. A little context goes a long way toward understanding reactions, needs, and emotions. If you know what they've gone through and where they are coming from, you'll be more likely to show compassion and patience rather than writing them off too quickly when facing unexpected behavior.

I'm not suggesting you ask invasive, personal questions about someone's past. That can become problematic not just on a social level, but on a human resources level as well. I'm simply saying that people's present is connected to their past, and the more you can become aware of their past, the better you'll understand their present. That is mostly up to them, though: the details they want to share are a personal choice, and the trust they grant you must be on their timetable and terms.

If you can, a good rule of thumb is to wait a few months before making any major decisions regarding someone you don't know that well: for example, before giving a person you've just hired a promotion, or handing a new volunteer a leadership role, or putting someone you haven't worked with in a critical decision-making position. That gives you time to move past the pleasantries and the honeymoon phase and get to know someone for who they really are. You can't rush people skills, and you can't accelerate building history.

On a related note, people who are considering taking a job with you or following your leadership in some other capacity are likely a bit hesitant about you as well—and that's a good thing. A recent study of two thousand job hunters found that the average job search took five months and included four different résumés, seven job applications, and five interviews.[4] People want to be in the right role and be connected to the right leaders just as much as leaders want the right people. So when you take the time to make sure people are a good fit or have the necessary qualifications for the role, it is to everyone's benefit. The better you know someone, the more effective you will be at serving and leading the person. Taking it slow is far better than making a rushed, poor decision that ends up hurting you, the person, and the team.

2. Build History Together

Working together over weeks, months, and even years, you will begin to build a shared history. You will learn to work together and to trust each other. This doesn't happen overnight, but it does happen, so don't be in too big of a hurry.

Building a shared history is important for several reasons. First, *it gives you time to learn how to work together*. You have a backstory too, and it influences your leadership. You also have a way of doing things that is uniquely you; you have a team, systems, structures, likes and dislikes, quirks and idiosyncrasies. The people you lead deserve time to get to know you

146

better as a person and a leader. They need to understand your leadership style and to find their place on the team.

To use another dating example, most relationship experts recommend taking a new relationship slow (not that anyone agrees on what "slow" means). At the very least, you probably don't want to declare your eternal devotion to the other person on the first date, even if you are sure you are head over heels in love. There's no rush. You're hoping to spend the rest of your life together, so you can at least wait for the second date—or the second year of dating—to start talking about love, marriage, and a baby carriage. It takes time for two people to mesh, to learn to walk together and work together and dream together.

In the same way, there is a benefit to taking organizational relationships slow: it gives everyone a chance to see how their skills, needs, and goals will fit together. You're in this for the long haul, so don't be in a hurry to fill every position on your dream team. Talk to people first and get a feel for where they've come from and where they are going. See if you really are compatible before you make major structural changes or put people in roles it would be hard to remove them from later.

Building a shared history is also important because *it prepares you for times of stress*. The leader-follower relationship rarely falls apart in the first two weeks, because real life hasn't set in yet. Use the first few months together to build trust, communication skills, and understanding of each other. That way you'll be prepared when tough times come: times of pressure, of stress, of hard work, of correction, of conflict. If you have a history together, you'll be more likely to believe in each other even when emotions run high or communication is less than perfect.

Finally, shared history *creates and protects long-term relationships*. We saw earlier that relationships are a key asset for leaders and organization. One of the best ways to build those relationships is simply by doing life together. Shared history is one of the greatest bonds a team can have, and it's a good reason to not easily give up on a relationship. The longer you've known people, the better you can predict their behavior and the more you can depend on each other.

As the pastor of a church, the shared history among our staff and volunteers is one of the things I am most proud of. Many of the original members

147

of our team, people who sacrificed time and effort to start a church in Los Angeles, are still with us. It hasn't been easy, but it is precisely those difficult moments, those challenges we faced together, that have knit our hearts together with a force far stronger than job descriptions or salaries.

3. Let Them Write Their Own New History

Letting people write history means not taking a snapshot of who they are now and holding them hostage to it forever. Give them room to create a new story. Human beings aren't static—they change. They grow, they improve, they mature, they develop. You change too, of course, and so does the world around you.

That goes for leadership, the workplace, volunteer organizations, churches and schools, families, or any other setting in which you might be exercising influence.

Because everyone's histories are still being written, you'll have to continually shift your understanding of people and their roles. You'll need to be aware of how they are changing both personally and professionally. Maybe when they started out with you, they were twenty-two, single, and willing to work all day and half the night. Now they have a spouse, two kids, a house, and precious little free time or extra energy. The fact that they don't answer your text messages at ten o'clock at night isn't a character defect or a lack of commitment: it's the reality of adult life and a better understanding of boundaries. In all likelihood, they make up for working fewer overtime hours by also making fewer mistakes, so allow your appreciation of their experience and wisdom to grow, and adjust your expectations of their availability.

The only constant in life is change.

This means you can't just arrange people in some perfect, ideal organizational chart and never think about their roles again. They are people, not objects, and they have free will and curiosity and dreams and opinions. Between their humanity and the tendency of organizational needs to change again and again, you will need to continually revamp your org chart. As a leader, your job is not to stack people like bricks in orderly rows. Your job is more like spinning plates. Or herding cats. Or chaperoning a middle school field trip. It's never still, never static, never finished.

As your team or organization grows and changes, people need to grow with it. Sometimes people can stagnate in their roles and be left behind by the changes in their organization. Part of your role is to encourage people to grow and adapt over time. If they aren't willing or able to change as needed, they may need to be moved into a different position. Ideally, though, their own growth will mirror that of the rest of the organization, fostering new talents and greater capacity in their own lives.

> When it comes to working with people, history matters.

Whether that is their history, your history, shared history, or future history (a bit of an oxymoron, I admit), a key part of working with people is to let time tell you what you need to know about them and how best to work together.

ooo

Thankfully, leadership is more than a swipe-left or swipe-right process. It's more than snap judgments and first impressions. You can (and must) truly know the people who are journeying with you. And as you do, you'll build something that goes far beyond a balance sheet or a profit-and-loss statement: you'll build a team of people who know and value and even love each other. It's worth taking the time to do it right, because together you are building each other and building the future.

KEY TAKEAWAY

Don't be in a hurry to make judgments about people's character or ability: get to know them first, and let time and shared history show you how to best work together.

EIGHTEEN

Listen to Lead

One of the most exhilarating pitches in baseball is the fastball. Fastballs average about 92 mph and make up nearly 60 percent of all pitches.[1] The current Guinness record holder for the fastest pitch is the Cuban-born pitcher Aroldis Chapman. In 2010, while playing for the Cincinnati Reds, he fired off a pitch that was clocked at 105.1 mph,[2] which pushes the limits of what the eye can even track. At speeds of over one hundred miles per hour, batters have about four-tenths of a second to see the ball, make a decision, and swing. That is, literally, the time it takes to blink.

Fastballs might be exciting, but they aren't the only pitch available to pitchers—and they're not always the most effective. There is another pitch, the changeup (also called the slow ball), that good pitchers use to throw batters off their game. At an average speed of 83 mph, and making up just 10 percent of pitches,[3] the changeup is meant to trick the batter into swinging too soon. Former professional pitcher Phil Rosengren says, "A good changeup can be a pitcher's best friend. Nothing frustrates a hitter more than a good changeup." Then he adds: "But the changeup can also be one of the toughest pitches to master."[4] Good pitchers know how to throw fast, but they also know how to slow things down with a changeup.

There is a similar dynamic in leadership communications. Most leaders have to be good at talking: in boardrooms, conference rooms, sales pitches, presentations, strategy meetings, speeches, phone calls, and one-on-one meetings. We mentor, correct, instruct, direct, and inspire, primarily using our voice. Talking is the most common pitch in our communication skill set. It's our fastball, and we use it all the time. But if *talking* is our fastball, *listening* is our changeup. It's another strategy to help accomplish our purposes. As a leader, you aren't on an opposing team trying to defeat those you engage with, so the baseball analogy only goes so far—I probably should have talked about choosing different tools from a toolbox when fixing a sink, or something like that. But I understand sports much better than do-it-yourself home improvement, so I'm going to stick with what I know.

Like a pitcher who switches between fastballs and slowballs, leaders who both talk and listen are able to engage their team in different ways. Talking to your team encourages them to listen and learn, but listening to your team teaches them to become active participants—not just in the conversation, but in the objectives of the team as well. Listening is an often overlooked but very effective way to lead your team, if you do it right.

Effective Listening

Effective listening is listening that accomplishes something. That might seem like a contradiction, because we often think of listening as passive. Talking, we might assume, gets things done, but listening is basically just waiting our turn to talk. That view does a disservice to listening, because we can often accomplish more by being quiet than we can by proclaiming our thoughts to the world. But for listening to be effective, we must listen with intention. Here are seven ways a leader can listen effectively in any conversation.

1. Listen to Serve

Listening effectively is, first of all, listening with an intent to serve. This deserves to be the underlying goal of most, if not all, dialogue or social interaction, but it is especially important in listening. Your goal is to help and serve people, and listening is the first step in figuring out how best to do that. Whether they are sharing an idea, a problem, a dream, a passion, or a story, be attentive to any way you might serve them better based on the information they are sharing.

When the conversation is about a pain point in someone's life, keep in mind that there is a difference between listening to fix and listening to serve. The first can actually be selfishness in disguise: maybe their confusion or hurt makes you uncomfortable, and you want to make it go away, so you give them a quick answer and try to move on quickly. Listening to serve, however, is empathetic listening. It means putting yourself in their place and trying to understand, to the best of your ability, the complexities of the problem. If you can give people an answer in two seconds to an issue they've been wrestling with for two weeks, be suspicious of your answer. It's probably too simplistic.

Even if you think you know the answer, you should still listen for a while and gauge where they are. They might not be ready for the answer, or they might resent the answer. Or, they might be too polite to tell you that your answer is actually terrible. If you sense defensiveness when you try to present ideas, it's often a sign to back off and listen more, because there is usually more to the story than what they've shared so far. Effective listening cares more about serving the person than expressing an opinion or finding a quick fix.

2. Listen to Develop the Relationship

Effective listening builds friendship and rapport. In a recent study, Harvard researchers examined what they called the "understudied conversational behavior" of asking questions. Asking questions is a sign of responsiveness in a listener, they theorized, and therefore a good indication of how well people listen. Their research identified "a robust and consistent relationship between question-asking and liking: people who ask more questions, particularly follow-up questions, are better liked by their conversation partners."[5] In other words, listening will make people like you more.

In one facet of the study, researchers looked at the conversational behavior of test subjects who were speed dating. Participants met in pairs for four minutes, conversed about whatever they desired, then moved on to the next partner. Speed daters who asked a higher number of follow-up questions during their dates were more likely to elicit agreement for a second date. (I'm just throwing that out there for anyone who might need it.)

The goal of leadership is not to get people to like you, of course—but it's certainly better than the alternative. Rather than trying to impress people with your clever conversation, your sense of humor, or your profound ideas,

Attentive listening will make you more relatable, more approachable, and more effective as a leader.

impress people by listening to them. Gain friends by asking questions. Build rapport with your team and your followers by expressing genuine interest in what they have to say.

3. Listen to Learn

Another way to listen effectively—maybe the most obvious one—is to focus on learning something you didn't know. Don't just wait your turn to talk, and don't just think about what you're going to say next. We all have friends like that—don't be that guy. Instead, pay attention to what people are saying and learn what you can.

As I mentioned earlier, make it your goal to keep the conversation centered more on the other person than yourself. Create an environment in which people feel comfortable being honest. Make a point of asking questions that draw out the other person's heart, ideas, and experiences. It's to your advantage to listen, because you don't learn anything new when you talk, but you almost always do when you listen.

What can you learn? Facts and information, to start with. But that's only the beginning. Truly listening is the best way to expand your horizons by being exposed to other worldviews, cultures, and perspectives. If you're a white male, for example, you'll never fully understand the experience of being a black woman, but listening closely, humbly, and empathetically to her stories will help you a great deal. You make your world bigger when you listen to other people.

4. Listen to Validate

Third, *listen to validate and respect the other person.* This is especially true as a leader, because your attention and time are valuable, and people know that. When you listen to people, you help them feel cared for, valued, and part of the team. Even if the "great idea" they are sharing with you is not actually that great, even if they are speaking mostly from emotion or immaturity, even if you aren't learning anything from them, take a few moments to listen. It's not a waste of time, because your attention is accomplishing something positive in *them.*

If you keep this goal in mind as you listen, you'll do more than just silently wonder if certain people will ever stop talking—a thought we've probably all had from time to time. Instead, you'll actively look for ways to affirm them, to validate them, and to encourage them during the conversation. Don't just listen passively or absentmindedly; be intentional about showing respect and value. That is effective listening.

5. Listen to Build Trust

Listening is one of the easiest and most effective ways to gain trust and the authority and respect that come with it. It's often been said that people don't care how much you know until they know how much you care, and listening attentively is a way of showing people that you care, that you are on their side, that you can be trusted. When you are a safe place to be honest, when you demonstrate that you care enough to listen, you gain trust and influence.

When you give people your complete and undistracted attention, you make relational deposits that will pay dividends of trust.

On the other hand, if you speak too soon, you can lose trust. For example, if you try to fix something before understanding it, or if you start throwing around blame, or if you say things like "I told you so," or "That was a dumb decision." A good leadership goal (and a good parenting goal, by the way) is to not be shocked by anything people say. Look beyond the venting, the blunder, or the

154

immaturity, and affirm the person. That's the first and most important step. Once trust is established, you can deal with the issue.

Listening to build trust, like listening to validate, must be intentional. You can't be scrolling through Instagram on your phone and expect people to open up about their dreams and fears.

6. Listen to Resolve Offenses

I hate to be the bearer of bad news, but your critics will multiply in proportion to your influence. The more you grow and the more you lead, the more likely you are to offend, disappoint, or hurt someone. It's not always possible (or even wise) to address the voices who criticize from a distance. But what do you do about those who are close to you, and what about your teammates or your organization's volunteers? How do you respond to people who follow you sincerely but were wounded by something you did or said (or something you *didn't* do or say)?

Often the best responses to a complaint or criticism is simply to listen, say thank you, and apologize if necessary. You don't always have to explain the nuances of your decisions or convince others why you are right. Listening can be an effective tool to calm emotions and give people a chance to express what they are thinking or feeling. Your willingness to listen will often help them, even if you don't necessarily take their suggestions or agree with their point of view. People need to speak their piece to find peace—some more often than others.

Actually, the fact that people feel strongly enough about something to face the negative emotions and potential fallout of challenging a leader says a great deal about their buy-in. That's incredible, if you think about it. Rather than resenting it, appreciate it. They are personally invested, they have made sacrifices, and they believe in the team. Their opinions matter to them, and they need to matter to you, even if you don't agree. Learn to see past the emotion and the exaggerations and to focus on the element of truth in what they want to convey. Usually, there is something you can learn from every complaint. To them, it's a mountain; to you it's a molehill. However, the reality is probably somewhere in between, and a little course correction on your part could actually be helpful.

7. Listen to Guide

Effective listening guides and teaches. Listening isn't just silence: you can ask questions, you can interject a few comments or ideas, and you can help people find answers on their own. It's interesting how much value ancient mentors and philosophers placed on listening to and dialoging with their students. Socrates was so well-known for teaching through questions and answers that his philosophy is known today as the Socratic Method. He asked questions in order to help his followers realize the superficiality of their knowledge and to make them dig deeper.[6] Jesus frequently answered people's questions with a question of His own, rather than just giving quick answers. Often His questions were meant to help people realize for themselves that they had a wrong view of God or of morality.[7] Confucius, Plato, Aristotle, and others all encouraged their disciples to learn through dialogue and exploration, rather than through rote memorization or top-down teaching.

People often want your ear more than your advice, so be quick to listen and slow to speak. Being invited to listen is not the same thing as being invited to give your opinion. A good leader knows the difference. There are times when people explicitly ask for help, but that's not always the case: don't assume that just because they are telling you their issues, they expect you to fix them. Many times, the mere act of talking through something, of processing an issue with a trusted confidante, will be enough for people to self-discover answers.

This protects you, because giving advice can be risky. Why? Think through the possible scenarios. First, if you give advice, they take it, and if it works, things are great and you are a hero, assuming they remember it was your advice (a big assumption). However, if they take your advice and it doesn't work, they'll probably blame you. And if they take your advice, do it completely wrong, and it doesn't work, they'll also probably blame you. Finally, if they refuse to take your advice, they will likely feel guilty about ignoring your counsel, which could affect the relationship as well. In three of the above four scenarios, giving advice didn't end well for the adviser. Just something to keep in mind.

Don't ever feel obligated to give advice, especially if you truly don't know what to do. Instead, listen. Ask probing, pointed questions. Help people come to their own conclusions. You'll actually earn trust equity with people if they know you won't make things up under pressure, and you'll help them find solutions that they truly believe in because they came up with them (mostly) on their own.

ooo

Learn to use the changeup pitch of listening. Don't do all the talking, even if you are good at it—which you likely are. Instead, strive to ask great questions, to pay attention to what gets people talking, to be fully present and engaged in conversations. Listening goes a long way toward winning with people and gaining leadership influence.

KEY TAKEAWAY

If you take time to truly listen to what people have to say, you'll win their trust, gain influence in their lives, and better serve their needs.

NINETEEN

One Conversation Away

A few years ago, researchers at Stanford University polled over two hundred CEOs, board directors, and senior executives of public and private North American companies. They wanted to learn what kind of leadership advice and influence their CEOs and top executives were receiving and what skills they were targeting for improvement. The highest-ranked area of concern among CEOs (nearly 43 percent) was conflict management skills.[1]

Stephen Miles, CEO of The Miles Group, which helped conduct the survey, stated, "How to manage effectively through conflict is clearly one of the top priorities for CEOs, as they are juggling multiple constituencies every day. When you are in the CEO role, most things that come to your desk only get there because there is a difficult decision to be made—which often has some level of conflict associated with it."[2] The study pointed out what most leaders have already experienced: conflict—and therefore conflict resolution—is a significant part of leadership. The study also pinpointed the answer: conflict management skills.

By "conflict" I don't necessarily mean a full-on fight, by the way. Conflict is usually more subtle and more complex than a shouting match over a conference table. A conflict is simply any situation in which two or more things are in opposition: conflicting opinions, conflicting decisions, conflicting values, conflicting personalities, conflicting budget proposals, and so on. We might call them disagreements, differences, or opposing views, but the bottom line is that two or more people are not on the same page with regard to a particular issue. And since teams and organizations by definition include more than one person, a certain level of conflict is to be expected. Leaders must know how to manage differences and disagreements of all kinds. They must have *faith* that conflict can be resolved and *courage* to engage in the necessary conversations.

In their book *Crucial Conversations: Tools for Talking When Stakes Are High*, author Kerry Patterson and his coauthors define a crucial conversation as "a discussion between two or more people where (1) stakes are high, (2) opinions vary, and (3) emotions run strong."[3] They go on to say that "when conversations matter the most—that is, when conversations move from casual to crucial—we're generally on our worst behavior." The authors also make this bold claim:

> At the heart of almost all chronic problems in our organizations, our teams, and our relationships lie crucial conversations—ones that we're either not holding or not holding well. Twenty years of research involving more than 100,000 people reveals that the key skill of effective leaders, teammates, parents, and loved ones is the capacity to skillfully address emotionally and politically risky issues.[4]

Nearly every conflict, every disagreement, and every offense is, in one sense, just one conversation away from being resolved. It has to be the right conversation, and the parties involved must have the right attitudes, as we'll consider below; but conflict does not have to continue unchecked, wreaking havoc on teams and destroying relationships. Conflict resolution is a people skill and a leadership skill you will use often.

Fighting Forward

As a leader, you might be involved in a conflict directly, or you might simply be trying to bring resolution among others who are at odds with each other. Either way, here's the main point to remember in any conflict, big or small: if handled properly, conflict can be both healthy and helpful. This is a basic philosophy of leadership that you should adopt, if you haven't already. Too often we try to avoid or quash conflict as quickly as possible; but if we realize that our disagreements, differences, arguments, and even fights are part of the growth process, we will approach them differently. We will use conflict to move us forward as a team and an organization.

Why do we so often try to escape or suppress conflict rather than using it to grow? There are at least three reasons. First, *we don't like the feelings that usually accompany it*. Disagreement is uncomfortable. It's awkward. It can cause difficult emotions such as sadness, fear, disappointment, and hurt. In a misguided and often subconscious attempt to avoid those emotions, we try to avoid the conflict that causes them.

Second, *we are afraid the whole thing will end badly*. The risks are real: ruined relationships, lost business deals, derailed meetings, lawsuits, and more. Those things might happen, of course, because the fact that conflict involves more than one party means you can't totally control the outcome. But conflict doesn't have to result in the worst-case scenario. Even in the dark, emotion-charged moments, there is a light at the end of the tunnel, and that light is reconciliation and growth. Don't let fear that conflict will produce drastic consequences keep you from facing a situation that needs to be addressed. Be wise, be cautious, be patient—but be brave as well.

Finally, *navigating conflict is hard work*. It takes time, effort, emotional strength, and mental investment. Sometimes it seems like it would be easier to just ignore differences and disagreements, but that approach is usually harder, not easier, in the long run.

So rather than avoiding or quelling conflict prematurely, make it work for you. How? By letting the discomfort motivate you to find solutions. Conflict almost always calls attention to an issue that needs to be addressed for the sake of long-term health. That issue could be a person, a problem, a system, a philosophy, or just about anything else. The point is that something is not right, and the painful feelings associated with conflict should spur you to figure out what that is. Just as physical pain motivates you to deal with things in your body you might otherwise let slide, so the emotional and mental pain caused by conflict can motivate you to fix whatever is wrong.

For example, conflict can prompt people to address their differences and find solutions that take both sides into account and are better as a result. It can alert someone that they have hurt or offended someone and encourage them to seek reconciliation. It can indicate a communication breakdown that needs to be addressed in order for things to work smoothly going forward. It can highlight differences in vision or philosophy that need to be resolved so the team can work together.

In addition to helping your organization grow, healthy conflict resolution will help you better fulfill your leadership role and goals. First, it *helps you serve people.* If people are your passion, you can't just lead them and believe in them when everyone is on their best behavior. If you can't love

> Properly handled, conflict will help your team or organization become more efficient and more effective by rooting out things that are hindering teamwork.

people at their worst, you can't lead them at their best. You have to preserve your relationships even when they aren't easy. Dealing with a conflict by ending a relationship is rarely the healthy thing to do.

Second, conflict resolution *helps you keep a clean conscience toward other people.* As much as possible, try to be at peace with everyone. That means not having unresolved offenses or ongoing feuds. You want to be able to run into people in the grocery store and not feel like you have to hide behind the tomatoes.

And third, resolving disagreements in a healthy way *helps you protect your reputation.* Your name is your greatest asset: it opens or closes doors. You don't want a reputation of being a leader who discards people who disagree with you. You can't leave a trail of bodies behind you and expect doors to open in front of you.

The goal of conflict resolution should be to improve and serve all parties involved: both the individuals at the heart of the disagreement or difference and the team or organization as a whole. If you learn to "fight forward," to handle conflicts properly, then even opposing opinions, contradictory beliefs, and painful misunderstandings can become catalysts for healthy change.

Four Steps for Handling Conflict Well

Handling conflict well does not mean sweeping issues under the rug as if they didn't happen and don't matter. It doesn't mean imposing your way on everyone around you by brute force. It doesn't mean pretending things are fine when they are not. It doesn't mean storming out of the room or cutting off the relationship. And it doesn't mean silently simmering until you explode and rain brimstone and lava down on everyone. None of those deal with the actual issue at hand.

Healthy conflict resolution means bringing closure to the issue at hand by addressing what needs to be addressed (communication), apologizing, if applicable (forgiveness), making changes (adjustment), and affirming the strength of the relationship moving forward (commitment). Let's look at each of these four points in more detail.

1. Communication: Address What Needs to Be Addressed

Every conflict is one conversation away from being resolved, as I mentioned above. It has to be the right conversation at the right time, and the participants have to be willing to work at it. Even deep misunderstanding or offense can begin to turn around when both parties sit down at the table and talk. Communication is about connection, empathy, and understanding. Words are the tools we use to communicate, but the goal is to truly understand the other person. It is to identify expectations and how those went unmet. It is to see things from the other person's perspective. It is to get everyone on the same side, working toward the same goal.

I'm not saying one conversation will make the hurt or confusion magically melt away, or that people will immediately become angels afterward. If the conflict has existed for months or years, you can expect to spend at least several weeks or months learning how to work in harmony again even after the issue has been addressed. But one honest, humble conversation can be the watershed moment, the first move in the right direction.

If the time isn't right or the other person isn't willing to pursue resolution, work on yourself. Even unresolved conflict can make you a better person if you're able to see past misunderstanding or differences and allow the situation to make you a wiser, more empathetic leader.

Often, the issue isn't really the issue. We've all experienced this. There have been times I've fielded a complaint from someone who was upset about a particular role they were given in an event or project, but the real issue wasn't the role: it was something deeper, usually an unmet expectation about their overall role in the organization. Taking the time to listen to their complaint was important, not because the specific pain point they brought up was so terrible in and of itself, but because it helped identify and deal with the heart of the issue. True communication happens when we take time to go beyond superficial issues and distracting debates and understand people's hearts.

2. Forgiveness: Apologize When Necessary

Apologies and forgiveness are not always necessary because not all conflict is a result of someone doing something wrong. But if there was some sort of offense, hurt, failure, betrayal, or any other harmful behavior, a sincere apology (and corresponding forgiveness) can work miracles. Remember, though, you can't insist someone apologize to you, and you can't demand someone forgive you. If apologies and forgiveness are not voluntary, they are not real.

That means that if you are even partly to blame, your focus should be on identifying, admitting, and apologizing for what you did, independently of whatever the other person may have done. For example, you could say, "I'm sorry I lost my temper. That was inappropriate and wrong." Period. End of sentence. Please do *not* add, "But it's your fault too, because you . . ." Apologies that have a "but" clause are excuses, not apologies.

Similarly, granting forgiveness is also independent of the other person. Yes, it is usually given in response to an apology—but not always. Ultimately, you choose whom to forgive and when to forgive them. Rather than waiting for an apology, try to find it in your heart to forgive. You would only be hurting yourself by holding on to bitterness or offense. Keep in mind that forgiveness is often more of a process than a onetime event. So many layers of emotion and need and motive are wrapped up in relational

163

conflict that it can be hard to sort out everything quickly. Even when you're committed to working things out, your own faults and motives may be revealed only slowly. As new layers of the issue come to light, choose to deal with them promptly, leaving the past behind and focusing on the future.

3. Adjustment: Make Changes

If the two people on either side of a conflict come to a resolution but don't make any changes, the issue is likely to blow up all over again. That's why the rug-sweeping trick never works: sooner or later, that rug gets pulled up, and the garbage from the past is still there. Change is the positive product of conflict, so don't avoid those tough conversations: seek them out and grow through them.

The reason conflict often produces growth is because it forces both parties to compromise, or better yet, to find a third option. The result is a solution that addresses the concerns of both parties, both of which usually have some validity. Rather than looking at conflict as two people butting heads over an issue, look at it as two people working side by side to solve an issue. The fact that you don't see eye to eye does not mean you are on different sides. You are a team, and there is strength in your diversity.

In this process of deciding what to adjust, focus on changing what you can, not what you can't. You can't change someone else's personality; you can't change the economy; you can't change certain limitations in your business, organization, or family. But you can always change your attitude. You can always grow in your own maturity, security, and integrity. And you can usually make changes to ensure that your organizational systems and policies are healthy and designed to benefit everyone for years to come.

4. Commitment: Affirm the Strength of the Relationship

Your end game should include relational growth: that is, a renewed commitment to the relationship and to the future. This is especially important if the conflict produced some level of hurt or offense. Conflict resolution hasn't happened if you just avoid each other from here on out. You might have to agree to disagree on some things or be willing to overlook certain quirks, but your bond will ideally be stronger, rather than weaker, after a conflict is resolved. A future together is stronger than a future apart, so make amends and move on.

Ultimately, these four steps—communicate, forgive, adjust, and commit—all point toward the same end: preserving valuable relationships and accomplishing shared goals. In other words, the focus of conflict resolution should be on the future and on what can be accomplished together once issues are resolved. Al-

As a leader, don't waste a good disagreement, and don't hide from a good conflict.

ways make conflict resolution more about the *resolution* than about the *conflict*. Don't obsess over the conflict: what caused it, how much it hurt, why it was totally unfair, who is to blame, and so on. Those things are important to some degree, but ultimately, the focus can't be the past. You are leading toward the future, and resolving disagreements, differences, and misunderstandings is an important people skill to develop along the way.

ooo

Waiting for you on the other side of conflict resolution and difficult conversations are stronger relationships, more unified teams, and greater commitment to the common goals.

If you can keep your cool and guide discussions wisely, you'll all come out better on the other side.

KEY TAKEAWAY

Conflicts and differences are a normal part of working together, and resolving them in a healthy manner will strengthen the team and organization.

---

ooo

Good people skills—whether manners or listening or communication or conflict resolution—are the key to winning with people. If you can master these things, you'll never lack for influence. People will follow you, people will receive from you, and people will be better because of you.

Learning to lead yourself (Part 1) and getting good at people skills (Part 2) are foundational to effective leadership. As we move into Part 3, our focus is on teamwork, the process of inspiring and influencing individuals to pursue a common goal.

PART 3

WE > ME

In Parts 1 and 2, we looked at the importance of leading yourself and developing people skills. Both are essential for leadership. Someone who is mature and self-aware but has zero people skills probably won't gather a team, no matter how great the person is, while someone with good social skills but no self-awareness or self-control might build a team, but it will likely implode once the pressure of leadership outgrows the character of the leader.

Both self-leadership and people skills are foundational for leadership, but they are not leadership in and of themselves because leadership requires a team. Character and charisma go a long way toward influencing others, but without a team, you won't be able to influence anyone beyond your direct reach. You will be your own lid.

If you are a healthy and growing *person* with effective *people skills* and you surround yourself with a strong *team*, your potential for influence increases exponentially. When you lead a team, you are the catalyst who mobilizes the influencers. You don't do everything yourself: you empower people to do more than you ever could, thus dramatically increasing your effectiveness. Your effectiveness is not in you, but in your team.

167

Leading teams and facilitating teamwork involves a skill set that, in some ways, is an extension of leading yourself and leading others. But the group dynamic associated with teams adds complexity and increases the stakes. It's not rocket science (unless the team you're leading actually works for NASA), and it's a skill set anyone can learn.

Part 3 addresses best practices for leading teams. Whether or not you have a title, and whether or not you receive a paycheck, you and your team will benefit from applying these principles to the day-to-day adventure of working together.

TWENTY

Let's Go!

In the climactic battle scene from *The Rise of Skywalker*, part of the *Star Wars* saga, commander and X-wing fighter pilot Poe Dameron tells his squadron that they aren't alone, and that good people just need good leaders.

The setting is typical over-the-top *Star Wars*: impossible odds, solar systems hanging in the balance, evil on the verge of winning. But it's actually a rather profound leadership statement. There are a lot of good people out there, more than we might realize, who want to make a difference and accomplish something significant. But unless they have a leader to follow—someone to inspire and guide the troops, someone to shout, "Let's go!" and then lead the way—it is unlikely they will come together as a team or step up to the challenge.

Part of the reason that *Star Wars* is so loved and so quoted (and has made so much money) is that it speaks directly to human experience. That is a bit ironic since the story is set in a distant galaxy and filled with alien creatures from exotic planets. Film critic Steven D. Greydanus says the films "offer rousing storytelling suffused by themes of moral struggle and transcendence . . . they give imaginative shape, albeit imperfectly, to basic human insights, and like the classical myths they have become a part of the cultural landscape."[1]

While Greydanus summarized the big-picture sweep of how the films focus on the human experience, Kirell Benzi, a self-described "data artist" with a PhD in data science, actually ran the numbers. Benzi researched the characters and species in the thirty-six-thousand-year timeline of *Star Wars* history, which includes not just the movie franchise but the expanded universe found in novels, comic books, video games, and more. Based on the (somewhat) definitive dictionary of all things *Star Wars*, fittingly named *Wookiepedia*, he counted a mind-boggling 21,647 characters. Of those, Benzi further studied the 7,563 most important characters, and he found that nearly 80 percent of them were human.[2] In other words, despite its otherworldly setting and extraterrestrial cast, *Star Wars* is about human behavior, human motivations, human struggles, human survival, human triumph. And woven throughout is the essential role of leadership in uniting people to fight for a common good.

Whether you love *Star Wars* or you wish the Sith would win once and for all and put you out of your misery, you can't escape the conclusion that humans, as a species, are well aware of their need to *follow* leaders and to *be* leaders. We idolize celebrities and mythologize heroes. We create Halls of Fame, we give awards, we track stats, we write biographies, we make movies. The need for leadership is ingrained not just in pop culture and mythology, but also in human existence, in our community structures, in the business world, in families, in churches, and in education.

People Need Leaders, and Leaders Need Teams

Good people need leaders if they're going to fight for a cause, work toward a goal, or win championships, but they don't accomplish those things alone—they do so in teams. People need leaders, but leaders need teams; and teams by definition work together, which is why so much of leadership is really about teamwork. Leadership expert Peter Northouse defines *leadership* as "a process whereby an individual influences a group of individuals to achieve a common goal."[3] Leadership is more than leading yourself, which is essentially self-discipline; and it's more than leading disconnected individuals, which is mentoring or maybe counseling. Leadership is leading multiple people who work together for the common good.

Northouse defines a *team* as "a type of organizational group that is composed of members who are interdependent, who share common goals, and who must coordinate their activities to accomplish these goals."[4] Each of those three phrases is important. Team members are *interdependent*: they rely on and serve each other. They have *common goals*: even if they have different strategies and personalities, they agree on where they are headed. And they *coordinate their activities*: they are intentional about getting all the moving parts to work together.

> Teams differ from groups primarily in the fact that they exist for a purpose.

Teams come in many forms and can be found in many areas of our lives. Some last for years; some last for days. Some have names and logos; some are ad hoc. Some work together in an office every day, and some connect via any number of technology tools.

They have a goal, or multiple goals, that team members are pursuing together. Groups share interests; teams share goals. Groups create relationship as an end in itself; teams create relationship with an end in mind. Teams have vision, direction, and momentum. They are going somewhere, and that means they need a leader to help them get there.

Chances are, you belong to multiple teams, and you might even lead or influence a few of them, whether or not you would formally define them as "teams."

- Family units are teams because they are pursuing the common goals of survival, personal growth (physical and emotional maturity), and numerical growth (future generations).
- School study groups or group projects are teams because they work together to get better grades or finish projects.
- Business or corporate environments often have multiple layers of teams, sometimes nested within or overlapping other teams, each tasked with managing or achieving a goal that moves the organization closer to achieving its mission.

- Churches, special interest groups, and other volunteer-based organizations create teams to achieve their objectives.

- Book clubs and hobby groups could be defined as teams because they intentionally extend the knowledge and experience of members in their area of focus.

- Neighborhood associations, watch groups, and block parties are teams that look out for the good of the greater community.

A defining characteristic of true teamwork is that *team* comes before *self*. That doesn't mean individual team members should sacrifice the entirety of their time, energy, and relationships to carry out the goal—martyrdom isn't a very sustainable leadership expectation. But it does mean that people buy in to a purpose or a goal that is bigger than themselves, and they are willing to do their part in achieving that objective. Leadership consultants and authors Gordy Curphy and Dianne Nilsen call this "buy-in," and they list it as one of the core elements of a successful team. They state:

> Buy-in happens when team members have a team-first, not a me-first, attitude. High-performance teams are committed to team goals, roles, and rules, and they're motivated to get necessary, day-to-day tasks done. They understand how their work contributes to the greater good, and they're optimistic about their chances of success.[5]

How can you determine if individuals are team players? Curphy and Nilsen recommend looking at whether or not they carry out team decisions. "If everyone in a team meeting agrees to a decision, but only some of the members change their behavior afterwards, then team commitment is not particularly strong."[6] Teamwork is not measured in emotions, speeches, titles, org charts, or promises—it is measured in actions.

This is first and foremost a heart issue. If people are truly part of the team, they will want to reach the team's goals, because those goals are *their* goals. They chose to be a part of the team, which means they have chosen to adopt and adapt to the values and objectives of the team.

That doesn't mean team members sacrifice their individuality on the altar of teamwork. In fact, it's often been pointed out that unity is not uniformity. Individuals can work well together and still be polar opposites in any number of ways: just ask most married couples. "Opposites attract" is real, and healthy teams embrace that dynamic and use it to their advantage. Diversity and differing opinions are a team asset, not a liability.

In team sports, the individuals' names usually go on the back of the jersey, but the team name goes on the front, and a team win is what each individual plays for. The team wins the trophy; the team gets the accolades; the team has the fan base; and the team will outlast the players. Individual contributions are important and should be celebrated but, ultimately, the best team players care about team wins, not credit for their individual contributions. I love how author and pastor Brian Houston describes the organization he built and leads, Hillsong Church, which is one of the largest and most influential churches in the world: he says it was "not built on the gifts and talents of a few, but on the sacrifices of many."[7]

> *Leaders who expect individuals to sacrifice for the team but balk at making any sacrifices themselves aren't team players.*

The same could and should be said for any successful team effort: it's about the many, not the few; and it's about the team, not the leader or the followers as individuals.

As a leader, you set the example by your own commitment to the greater good.

As a leader, being a team player means you are willing to lay down your pride, your comfort, your success, and your fame for the team when necessary. Your team will follow your lead. If the cause is important enough for you to make sacrifices, your people will do the same.

This selfless, leadership-by-example approach is a key factor in successful teams because it keeps leadership and people connected. Leaders need people, so they must be humble and service-oriented; and people need leaders, so they must be willing to contribute their part to the team's overall goals. People need leaders, and leaders need teams. So when a good leader builds a great team, it's a win for everyone.

Three Components for Successful Teamwork

Good leaders and great teams are the foundation for success, but that doesn't mean positive results happen immediately or automatically. They are the result of strategic leadership and committed teamwork that relies on three basic components: direction, people, and systems.

1. Direction: Know Where You Are Going

Some people might have team buy-in regardless of the objectives of the team or organization because they trust you and are loyal at heart. But most long-term team members need buy-in not just to you as a leader, but also to where you are going. They must believe in the direction the team is headed. Direction is both long-term and short-term. Long-term direction is often described with terms like "vision" or "mission," while short-term direction might be called "strategy," "goals," or "objectives." Know where you are going, both short-term and long-term, and communicate that.

For example, I've done a speaking tour called Hope Is Here on a couple of different occasions. It's a multi-city event with music, performances, and an inspiring message at the end. The goal of the event is to build people's hope, faith, and courage. We have a clear *direction* for the tour. It's not a conference, or a teaching event, or a worship night, or an old-school revival meeting—it's a night of inspiration. Everything we do is built on that premise and works toward that goal. Our clarity of direction empowers our team to exercise creativity within a defined framework and unites our efforts around a clear goal.

2. People: Know Whom You Need

Once you know your direction (both long-term and short-term), you'll be better equipped to decide which people to have on the team and where they best fit. Whether you are creating a research and development team for a new product, deciding whom to send to open a new business location, or determining whom to have on your board of directors, your direction will determine your team.

174

On a side note, these two things—direction and people—influence each other, meaning that there will be times when your direction will be determined, in part, by your people. In other words, as an organization, you can and should play to the strengths of the people who are already on your team. We'll take a closer look at the connection between people and vision in a later chapter.

Whom you choose depends to a great extent on ability, of course, since people have to be able to do the job at hand. But many other things might come into play as well, including their integrity, work ethic, loyalty, personality, past experience, and more. It's about having the right people on board and having them in the right place, too.

On our Hope Is Here tour, the direction determined our personnel needs: we had to hire bus drivers, musicians, tour coordinators, caterers, and more. Dozens of people in each city helped make the events a success, and the reason they worked together so well was because each person's role was aligned with the overall purpose and direction of the tour.

3. Systems and Structure: Know How to Get Where You're Going

Healthy organizational structure is a lot like your skeleton—you don't usually notice it unless something is broken, and then it hurts like crazy. People can rarely function at their best in dysfunctional environments, and it will be hard for your team to run well if your systems and structure are broken or off-balance. Organizational systems and structure aren't optional, but neither are they impossible—and they might be all you lack to take your team to the next level.

Our Hope Is Here tour had a clear direction and stellar team, but it was the underlying *systems* that allowed us to function smoothly from city to city. Every morning we woke up in a different location and held our events in a different venue, but the procedures were the same. There were clear policies for everything from bunk area cleanliness to tour bus restroom etiquette. A production crew set up early in the morning, tape on the floor guided people to the right areas during the event, and tickets sales and child sponsorship stats were available in real time on an app. From start to end, well-thought-out systems helped coordinate the work of multiple people to carry out the vision of the tour.

Moving in the right direction, with the right people, supported by the right systems, will go a long way toward creating productive leadership. If you find yourself frustrated with a lack of progress in an area under your leadership, take a closer look at all three of these issues. Do you have a clear, well-communicated direction? Are the right people in the right places? And are your systems supporting and empowering those people to do their jobs and achieve the team's goals? We'll look at systems in greater detail in a later chapter, because a few small adjustments in these areas can often make all the difference.

ooo

Whether you are building a business or saving the galaxy, there are few things more exhilarating, more rewarding, and more motivating than knowing that, day after day, you get to pursue a cause you care about with people you trust. Leadership and teamwork, when they are done right, create a team experience that is both effective and exciting. Be the leader who inspires like-minded people to work together, who shouts, "Let's go!" and leads people toward their future.

KEY TAKEAWAY

Leaders need teams and teams need leaders, so lead your team in a way that accomplishes goals and advances team vision together.

TWENTY-ONE

What Do We Want?

Kallie Dovel, Alli Swanson, Anna Toy, Brooke Hodges, and Jessie Simonson were typical college juniors, enjoying campus life while trying to decide what they wanted to do after graduation. Kallie had recently returned from a trip to Uganda, where she met women her own age who were single moms, without education or jobs, who had grown up in a war-ravaged country. To survive, the women created jewelry, using paper beads they recycled from old posters, which they sold to the few tourists who came through. Kallie brought some of the jewelry back home with her, and it was an instant hit with her friends.

The five college friends had an idea: maybe they could help these women, and others as well, by providing a larger market for their products. That meant jumping into the world of international business, studying fashion trends, bridging cultural barriers, and understanding social and economic development. It was, in their words, "the beginning of the hardest, scariest, and most incredible journey imaginable."[1] As Simonson told *Forbes* magazine in an interview, "We were college girls who had never run a business, let alone a business in Africa."[2]

That didn't stop them. They were determined not only to provide dignified employment to women in Uganda, but also to change lives. And today, less than fifteen years later, they are doing just that. They employ previously abused and underserved women in Uganda, and they provide them with income, education, financial training, business mentoring, and healthcare for five years. Their company, 31 Bits, supplies jewelry to over 350 stores, including large retail outlets such as Nordstrom, and they've been featured in *Forbes*, *Harper's Bazaar*, and *Elle*. They have expanded into multiple locations and countries, including Indonesia and Bali, and their product line features not just an extensive line of jewelry, but also handbags, home goods, and more.

The company has been a pioneer in providing environmentally friendly, responsibly sourced products. They were among the first "give-back" companies, and their business model has always been about empowering their providers, not just making a profit. Since their beginnings, they have been on the forefront of raising awareness of the need for ethical fashion, educating consumers about the impact of their purchases.

Forbes states that the five friends are "clear on what success looks like for them: rather than a one-for-one model, or giving back a percentage of their projects, they have focused on getting their artisans independent in five years." That means they continually lose their best-trained employees and have to start over. But as Simonson said in the interview, "We always wanted these women to be out there working, setting up their own businesses, and sustaining themselves. After all, that's sustainability, isn't it?"

The story of 31 Bits is an inspiring illustration of social enterprise: a business model with both financial and social goals. Social enterprises address needs or solve problems in the world around them through a market-driven approach.[3] This wholistic attitude toward business is gaining popularity because many people want more than a profitable bottom line: they also want to do good and to help others, but in a financially sustainable way.

Defining Success

The five friends who formed 31 Bits understood the importance of being clear on what success looks like for you and your team: in their case, success was providing dignified employment leading to financial independence for disadvantaged women. Every team or organization, no matter the size, must answer the question, "What do we want?" In other words, they need to be clear on their vision and their definition of success.

178

If you don't define success beforehand, you and your team run two risks. First, you can be lulled into *inadvertent complacency* by a false sense of progress. You might feel like you're doing well, but feelings are notoriously unreliable. Without a predefined, objective way to measure progress, you can coast along on minimal effort—and produce minimal results. Having no established goals means no accountability; and no accountability allows complacency and even laziness to set in. You can subtly create an environment that values things like camaraderie, team spirit, and unity, but undervalues actually getting work done.

> Knowing what you want, both as a leader and as a team, will drive every decision you make.

The second risk of undefined success is *unfocused busyness*. In other words, your team might do a lot of work in a lot of areas, but since there is no cohesive direction, you don't really move forward—you just keep busy. Henry David Thoreau wrote in a letter to a friend: "It is not enough to be industrious; so are the ants. What are you industrious about?"[4] In other words, what is the goal of your busyness? That is the question every leader and team must ask, because busyness is not always connected to vision. What future are you aiming for, and how do you plan to get there? Define your vision, *then* get busy. You'll go further, and you'll get there faster.

Defining what you want as an organization will help you avoid the twin traps of inadvertent complacency and unfocused busyness. But it will do more than that: it will help you chart a course that is practical and reachable by breaking your *vision* down into bite-size *wins*.

Vision and Wins

I like to answer the "What do we want?" question in terms of both vision and wins. There are a lot of words thrown around in leadership that relate to the future: mission, goals, mileposts, steps, stages, phases, objectives, purposes, targets, aims, intentions, focuses, and plans, to list a few. There is considerable overlap in the definitions of these terms, and most teams choose their own terminology to describe the journey they are on. For me, though, vision is the *long-term objectives* of the team, including who you are and why you exist, and wins are the *short-term, tangible accomplishments* along the way.

1. Vision: Long-Term Objectives

Defining your vision requires answering the "What do we want?" question clearly and boldly. Vision is usually painted with broad strokes. It's not just what you do, it's who you are and who you want to be. It's a dream you see in the distance, something to aim for and work toward. Often it is described using superlatives: "to make the best shoe on the market," "to provide the greatest selection of watches in the world," or "to be a church where everyone belongs." The size of the dream makes it inspiring, even contagious. People respond to the vision you see in your head and paint with your words.

Vision has a sense of *destiny* to it, a sense of calling. It's not just a business or a job, it's a calling. You might say things like, "I was born for this," or "I would do this even if I wasn't paid for it," or "I know we can do this." You find yourself talking about it with anyone who will listen. You stay up at night thinking about it, brainstorming ways to make your vision a reality.

Vision has a sense of *challenge* to it as well. Hence the superlatives—you want your organization and team to be the best. You want to do what no one else has done before. It's not a fanciful dream, but it's not a walk in the park, either. If it were easy, someone else would have done it already, but you believe you are up to the challenge.

Strategies come and go, but vision changes only slowly, if at all.

Vision also has a sense of *permanency* to it. It's a goal in the distance, one you use to align your efforts and measure your progress—often for years to come. It's what you and your team go back to when you are discouraged by resistance or obstacles along the way.

It stands always a little way into the future, beckoning, encouraging, challenging.

The difference between vision and mission, or between a vision statement and a mission statement, is also defined by each leader and team. Not everyone agrees on the difference, which is totally fine. For me, vision

180

is a reflection of mission. That is, our vision describes how we implement our mission. Our mission as a church, for example, is an overarching statement of why we exist: "to help people know God, find freedom, discover their gifts, and make a difference." Our vision, on the other hand, is more practical and visible: we want to spread a message of love and hope in our city, we want to open church locations in other cities, and much more.

Regardless of the terms you use, the point is that you must have a long-term approach to your organization's goals. Where do you want to be in five, ten, or twenty years? If you look far down the road, what do you see for your team, your organization, and yourself?

2. Wins: Short-Term Accomplishments

It is important for leaders to be clear about the difference between vision and wins. For example, imagine you gather everyone together and share your dream in grand, dramatic terms. You talk about changing lives, about innovating, about risk-taking, about disruptive products and services, about capturing market share. You give a motivational speech worthy of an Oscar and send people back to their desks feeling energized and excited. But three months go by and you realize nothing has changed—you're no closer to realizing your dream, and no one even remembers your motivational speech. You can't help but wonder, *Why aren't people getting it?*

What happened? You cast a great vision, but you didn't identify any wins, any short-term goals. Vision is bold, grand, inspiring—and somewhat generic. It has to be, because it encompasses a future that might take years to become reality. In contrast, wins are *now*, or at least in the near future, and they are specific steps that put feet to vision.

"Vision without implementation is hallucination," someone once said, and wins are the progressive implementation of vision. Your team's vision might be to redefine the industry, but a win would be to launch three new products this year, or to land a feature in an industry magazine, or to eliminate 60 percent of waste during the production process, or anything else that takes you one step closer to your vision.

Maybe your team doesn't need a tearjerker motivational speech about your thirty-year plan as much as they need weekly sales goals. Maybe telling

181

your startup about your dream of world domination should be followed by simpler goals that you hope to accomplish in the next three months, such as getting your website up, setting up accounting procedures, and purchasing office furniture. These tasks may be more mundane than world domination, but people tend to appreciate big dreams more when they are accompanied by practical steps to accomplish them.

Vision is inspiring and essential, but measurable, achievable milestones are a much better source of ongoing motivation. Confusing the two is where leaders frequently fail and why teams often get frustrated. Leaders have to routinely break down long-term vision into short-term wins. Your team needs to know what to strive toward not just over years and decades, but also in weeks, months, and quarters.

A win is any measurable goal: something you can attain over the course of weeks or months, or the progress from one year to the next. For example, you might define a win as reaching $1 million in quarterly sales, going ninety days without accidents on the job, or growing your social media following by 200 percent.

In order to track wins, you have to define them; and in order to define them, you have to decide what is important to you. Again, it comes back to answering the question, "What do you want?" You have to decide where you are going long-term, then decide what you can do right now to take steps in that direction. Those steps are your wins.

So, how do you decide what steps to take? How do you know what a win looks like for you and your team? To start with, take a look at what you measure. If you claim something is important but you don't measure it, it's probably not really that important to you. Conversely, if you think you don't care about something, but you find yourself tracking it, it's probably more important than you care to admit.

For example, in the church community I lead, we have a weekly "Monday Report" that summarizes the metrics we track from our Sunday gatherings and, when applicable, compares them to the previous year on that date. We record attendance, donations, number of vehicles in the parking lot, volunteers, load-in and load-out time at our venue, live-streaming viewers, and more. The Monday Report is a quick way for my team and me to see where we are winning, or seeing progress, and where we need to continue to grow.

If something actually is important to you but you aren't measuring it, figure out how to start. That's not always easy, but it's incredibly helpful if you can do it. How else will you know if you are winning or losing? You might be doing better than you think, but you'll never know until you find a way to benchmark progress. A leader and a team that don't know if they are winning or losing are losing by default: even if they are making some progress, they can't be the best version of themselves because they don't know where they really are or where they need to improve. They will lose opportunities and momentum because they have lost themselves.

Metrics is simply another term for measurement. It refers to measurable, trackable stats that help organizations evaluate their progress. George Forrest, writing for business services company iSixSigma, states that "Metrics are used to drive improvements and help businesses focus their people and resources on what's important."[5] Notice the positive focus of that explanation: numbers bring improvement and focus. Numbers are your friend, even if they aren't the numbers you were hoping for, because they quantify progress and help a team focus on what's important.

Never avoid metrics just because you're afraid of what you'll discover. It's better to find out now where you stand or what you're walking into rather than being caught by surprise later. Good leaders can't always avoid hard times or bad news, but they can be as prepared as possible beforehand. Forrest continues, "Fudging metrics benefits no one. To deliver real progress, everyone involved with the metric needs to be completely honest. . . . Understanding the company's true position is the first step toward improving it."[6]

As a leader, you can't be everywhere all the time, so the decisions you make will inevitably come from a combination of data and people. People give you subjective feedback, which has its place, but data gives you objective feedback you can use to make informed decisions. Both objective and subjective sources of input are important, and together they give you confidence in your decisions. Seek accurate information, regardless of what it tells you, and make informed choices.

I have to do this from time to time with our employees. Like any organization, we evaluate people periodically based on their performance: they have benchmarks to hit, goals to meet, and jobs to accomplish, and we usually have data that provides an objective picture of their job performance. But data can never tell the whole story. Sometimes people are going through personal issues, or outside factors kept them from reaching their goals this quarter. Maybe they were recently given a new area of responsibility and are still struggling with the learning curve. As a leader, you can't just look at the cold, hard facts—but you can't ignore them either. Get knowledge, but also get understanding. That is, evaluate the data, but then look below the surface to identify what is really going on before making any drastic decisions.

Remember, *you* as the leader define your wins, along with others on your leadership team. You decide what you want. Don't get sidetracked chasing someone else's definition of a win. Of course, you should allow yourself to be informed by what others are doing or pursuing, but you and your team are unique. You can only be really good at a few things, so be really good at the things you *want* to be good at, and celebrate the wins that get you there.

When identifying wins, take into account the makeup of your team, your resources, and your situation; and do your best to keep the wins achievable. Be realistic about what you can accomplish; there's no point in discouraging your team by throwing out random numbers everyone knows are too grandiose. Since vision is, by definition, long-term, and therefore progress won't always be immediately obvious, your wins need to be easy enough and often enough that your team can observe its advance.

The more wins you can define, the better. Sports teams have a very visible win-loss record for their games, but games aren't the only wins they track. They are also looking for things like player improvement, greater teamwork, ticket sales, positive off-the-field behavior, merchandise sales, a growing fan base, and more. In your organization and with your team, find ways to set attainable goals and create opportunities for frequent success. More opportunities for success means that more people will be involved in winning—and that's always a good thing.

ooo

The clearer your vision and the more measurable your wins, the greater the odds that you and your team will soon feel the wind at your back. It

184

won't always be easy, of course. But when your resources are aligned with your purpose, and when you have clearly defined steps to take each day, progress is natural and almost inevitable.

KEY TAKEAWAY

Decide what you want to achieve as a team and then measure, track, and celebrate wins along the way.

TWENTY-TWO

Chemistry and Culture

A recurring motif in fairy tales and myths is the infamous love potion: a mysterious, magical elixir meant to make the object of the bearer's affection fall in love with him or her. There are two problems with that, of course: first, there's no such thing as a love potion. Second, it's creepy, invasive, and borderline assault. In most fairy tales and myths, the potion backfires in some way, and the moral of the story is always the same: true love can't be manipulated—it must be freely given.

While there is no such thing as a potion to make someone fall in love with you, science has identified aspects of the brain—in particular, certain chemicals and hormones—that are associated with love and other relationship factors. Whether that knowledge could (or should) be leveraged to remedy unrequited love remains to be seen. But understanding the chemistry of relationships has practical and very beneficial implications not just for jilted lovers but for leaders and teams as well.

Helen Fisher is a biological anthropologist whose research on the brain systems behind personality, attraction, and love has been featured in academic journals, conferences, and business relationship studies. Her research has also been of interest to the dating website Match.com, and it's not hard to see why. A dating website that could predict or even enhance compatibility would be the millennial version of a love potion. When the website asked Fisher why one person falls in love with another, she turned to neurology.

She said, "I spent two years studying the literature and found, over and over, that four biological systems—dopamine/norepinephrine, serotonin, testosterone, and estrogen/oxytocin—are each linked to a particular suite of personality traits. I found this in research not only on humans but also on doves, lizards, and monkeys."[1] She went on to apply her research to relationships in general, not just romantic pairings, and her work is a foundational element in an innovative personality assessment developed by Deloitte called Business Chemistry. More about that in a moment.

According to Fisher, the dopamine system is linked to people who tend to be curious, creative, spontaneous, and risk-takers. High serotonin activity is found in people who are sociable, eager to belong, and often more traditional in their values and less inclined toward curiosity. The testosterone system is linked to characteristics such as being tough-minded, direct, and decisive. Finally, the estrogen and oxytocin systems are correlated to people who tend to be more intuitive, imaginative, trusting, and empathetic.

While all of this is fascinating, it doesn't mean that brain chemistry *controls* us, of course, nor does it give us license to label people or put them in a box. Brain chemistry and personalities are tendencies, not taskmasters, and other factors such as culture, environment, background, values, and morals come into play as well. But chemistry does *influence* behavior and personalities in ways that have potential implications for leadership. For example, understanding a little more about how the brain works could help you to value rather than resent people on your team who are different, and to invite their participation in areas where you are weak rather than feeling threatened by their strengths.

Team Chemistry

While personalities are affected by literal chemistry, the idea of team chemistry goes beyond just the physical or emotional makeup of people. It refers to how individuals with unique personalities and abilities merge into a cohesive unit. Good team chemistry means getting along and working together.

Each person has an understanding of how to interact with others on the team in a healthy and productive way.

The Business Chemistry framework developed by Deloitte—which is based on Fisher's analysis of neurological influences in relationships—identifies various work styles and provides tools and research to show how teams can work together better. Deloitte's researchers have found that when teams consistently underperform, team members themselves are rarely to blame. Rather:

> [The fault] rests with leaders who fail to effectively tap diverse work styles and perspectives—even at the senior-most levels. Some managers just don't recognize how profound the differences between their people are; others don't know how to manage the gaps and tensions or understand the costs of not doing so. As a result, some of the best ideas go unheard or unrealized, and performance suffers.[2]

In other words, a good leader is aware of the various personalities around the table and knows how to take advantage of diversity, rather than ignoring it or being confused or frustrated by it.

Chemistry doesn't mean there will never be arguments or disagreements, and it doesn't mean everyone has to feel warm fuzzy feelings about each other all the time. That's not realistic or healthy. If you always get along, it may even be an indication that the team is too homogenous. Invite diverse opinions and perspectives into the room—you'll be stronger because of it.

When teams have the right chemistry, individual members don't value others despite their differences but because of their differences.

Chemistry is less about agreement and more about commitment. You can choose to be compatible with colleagues you might not naturally gravitate toward as friends. You might never go on vacation together or take selfies together, but that doesn't mean you can't work well together—after all, being work friends is better than being work adversaries. And over time, as you share experiences, overcome obstacles, and build something together, you might even develop a bond that becomes a long-term friendship.

When it comes to building a team, chemistry is not the only factor, but it's an important one. I always look for what I call the four Cs: *chemistry, character, competence,* and *capacity.* All four are important. Chemistry can't be the sole basis that gets someone a spot on a team, but on the other hand, neither can competence. You need chemistry to work together, character to stay true and act with integrity, competency to get the job done well, and capacity to handle the pressure that will come. Of the four, chemistry might be most easily overlooked because we tend to assume a great worker will be a great team member. Often that's true, but it's not a given.

A Word about "Bad Chemistry"

Don't give up too quickly on a team member who appears to have "bad chemistry"—that is, if they don't seem to mesh quickly with the team or they have very different ideas. Often, the awkwardness or conflicts aren't due to a character defect, but to differences in education, culture, or habit, and the team member will change with a little bit of patience. Or, the lack of chemistry might indicate that the person isn't in quite the right place on the team yet, and you need to make some adjustments. People are your most valuable resource, and letting them go should be a last resort. For one thing, you're working with humans, not machines or a carpet that can be swapped out for another with no repercussions. People have feelings, needs, families, financial commitments—and, if they work for you, employment rights. Rather than chopping people off who don't easily get along, first evaluate where the fault lies.

Sometimes "bad attitude" and "bad chemistry" can be terms leaders use to justify getting rid of someone who sees things differently and is willing to speak up for the good of the team. Challenging the status quo, asking direct questions, or pointing out potential problems in a plan is not bad chemistry. People with different opinions are advantages you should seek, not voices you should silence. Of course, when people are *always* the devil's advocate, or when they don't change aggressive or subversive habits even after repeated confrontations, it may well be in everyone's best interests (theirs included) for them to move on. But again, that's a last resort, because letting people go who were brave enough to express an opinion that contradicted yours or that ruffled a few feathers only teaches the rest of the team to suppress any contradictory truths or opinions so they don't lose their jobs, too.

In his book *Am I Being Too Subtle?*, billionaire businessman Sam Zell says his "greatest fear is not having information that might protect me from making a mistake."[3] His solution? Create an environment in which information flows freely and people have direct access to leaders. He says he didn't even realize the office he had used for thirty-five years had a door until he was remodeling it, because he had a literal open-door policy: it was literally always open. "Everyone is welcome in my office, from senior executives to the person in the mailroom," he writes. "By extension, if the number one guy is totally accessible, then anyone else who isn't looks like a schmuck." He strongly advocates for people to speak up when they have a concern. "I tell people 'No surprises' and I mean it. I'm confident enough to believe that if I catch a problem early on, we'll be smart enough to fix it. So, *don't hide things. Relax. We don't kill the messenger around here.*"[4]

Your challenge in leadership is to differentiate between people who cause problems and people who recognize problems—and it's not as easy as you might think. Sam Zell isn't afraid people will express dissenting opinions: he is afraid they will *hide* them, and he'll miss out on valuable feedback. It's a great principle to live by, and it's why you should be "quick to listen, slow to speak, and slow to get angry" to quote an ancient Bible author (James 1:19 NLT). Invite as many perspectives as you can, listen to as many opinions as possible, and learn to incorporate diverse personalities into your team. If you can understand—and learn to utilize—the chemistry of your team, the effectiveness of your organization will usually grow proportionally.

Team Culture

Closely connected to team chemistry is the concept of team culture. Culture exists in a team whether you intentionally create it or not. Similar to the culture of a country or ethnic group, team culture refers to the (usually) unwritten rules of conduct that set the atmosphere and permeate every interaction within a team or organization. It is a set of shared values and behavioral expectations that empower teams to work as cohesive units.

Culture trumps virtually everything else in an organization. Management consultant Peter Drucker puts it this way, "Culture eats strategy for breakfast."[5] Why? Because culture isn't what you do or what you say, but who you are; and who you are—as a leader, as a team, as an organization—always comes through eventually.

Team culture can be broken down into three things: vision, values, and standards. *Vision*, as we saw in the previous chapter, refers to where you and your team are going long-term. It is a broad picture of who you are and who you want to be as an organization. Vision is a goal with heart. *Values* are the things you uphold as most important. They usually come from and support your vision. These are the nonnegotiables that you defend and preserve no matter what. *Standards* are the high bars you set for performance and behavior as you carry out your vision. They articulate what you expect, even demand, from your team.

These three things—vision, values, and standards—can be very specific. For example, our church's vision includes communicating our message of faith and love to as many people as we can. Since our *vision* is to communicate well, we *value* communication tools, especially technology, and we invest the time, money, and attention necessary to carry out that vision. Likewise, we have high *standards* in our audio, video, and other creative departments because excellence in those areas contributes to accomplishing our vision. Both our standards and our values reflect and support our vision.

Keep in mind that culture isn't about right or wrong but about team unity and about facilitating chemistry, as we saw above. Culture is always about *we, our,* and *us,* rather than about *me* or *you.* This is how *we* do things. This is how *we* talk to each other. *We* don't use words like that. *We* handle conflict like this. *Our* values are such and such. *We* respond to complaints this way.

Me can be selfish and *you* can be accusatory, but *we* is inclusive. *We* points to teamwork, and that's the point. That's the ultimate goal of both chemistry and culture, after all: a team that is united in heart, in word, in vision, and in action.

Establishing a healthy team culture has many benefits. It enables individuals to work together in unity. It encourages people to feel part of a larger unit. It establishes a yardstick for evaluating the behaviors, attitudes, and decisions that are encouraged or discouraged in the organization. It facilitates the onboarding of new hires or new volunteers by providing a congruent environment that naturally teaches them what is expected of them. It provides a subtle peer pressure—the good kind—that encourages highly individualistic people to stay (relatively) in bounds. It helps reduce or avoid conflict by providing a set of ground rules. I could go on, but you get the point: taking the time to build the right culture will serve you and your team in many ways.

Because who you are will always come through eventually, you can't fake culture. This is especially important for leaders to keep in mind. You can't just talk about, teach about, complain about, or dream about the culture you want—you have to *be* that culture, both as a leader and as a team. That means that one of your responsibilities is to embody your culture in everything from the way you greet people in the hallway to the way you make decisions and allocate budgets. It also means you must help others reflect that culture as well.

You have to become the culture you want because culture is caught, not taught. It is observed, not imposed. It's what you *actually* do, not what you say you do, or what you think you do, or what's written on your wall or website. It is partly a reflection of the leader, partly a reflection of the team, but mostly a reflection of what is rewarded, tolerated, or reprimanded over the course of time.

Ultimately, you as a leader are responsible for the culture of your team. That means no matter what things look like now, you can turn the ship around. If you don't like what you see, you have the power to change it. More than anyone else, you are best equipped to establish, model, and monitor culture. Hold others—and hold yourself—accountable to the culture you want to propagate.

ooo

You don't have to be an anthropologist-turned-brain-guru like Helen Fisher to understand that chemistry and culture are an invisible—yet incredibly powerful—part of building teams and carrying out vision. As the leader, you can use them both for the good of the people you lead. A little understanding and a lot of consistency is all it takes to build your team's unity and multiply their effectiveness.

KEY TAKEAWAY

Be aware of the chemistry among your team members and the culture that permeates your organization, and be proactive about achieving the healthiest, most unified team possible.

TWENTY-THREE

Influencing the Influencers

ccording to British journalist Paul Vallely, the earliest documented marketer to take advantage of influencers was a late-nineteenth-century French chemist named Angelo Mariani.[1] Mariani became intrigued with coca, the plant from which cocaine is extracted, and its economic potential after reading an Italian neurologist's paper that described coca's effects. The coca leaf had been part of Inca life for thousands of years, where it was used as a stimulant, often in religious, ceremonial, and medicinal contexts. It entered Spanish and eventually European cultures after their invasion of the Americas, and it became popular for its supposed medicinal effects.

In 1863, Angelo Mariani developed Vin Mariani, a coca wine made from Bordeaux wine and coca leaves. Vin Mariani was 11 percent alcohol and contained over 6 milligrams of cocaine in every ounce, and the ethanol in the alcohol reinforced the effect of both drugs. Naturally, it became both popular and profitable, and others started manufacturing similar beverages. At the time, cocaine's addictive properties had not been discovered.

Mariani's real innovation, however, was not Vin Mariani, but his marketing strategy. According to Ryan Kucey of Better Marketing, Mariani managed to secure as many as four thousand testimonials from a wide range of European celebrities and household names, which he then printed as advertisements in newspapers and magazines. Jules Verne, Alexander

Dumas, Sir Arthur Conan Doyle, Robert Louis Stevenson, Queen Victoria, King George of Greece, King Alfonso XIII of Spain, the Shah of Persia, US presidents William McKinley and Ulysses S. Grant, and even Pope Leo himself were said to have tried the product. According to an advertising poster produced by Mariani, the pope even awarded him a gold medal and wrote that he "fully appreciated the beneficent effect of this Tonic Wine."[2]

Interestingly, another brand famous for its advertising prowess in the late 1800s also relied on coca. In America, shortly after Prohibition began, an Atlanta pharmacist took the recipe for a popular caffeine-infused coca wine and replaced the wine with sugar syrup. He named it Coca-Cola.

For a time, cocaine-infused products were sold over the counter in pharmacies and stores such as Sears and Harrods of London. Even Sigmund Freud extolled the benefits of cocaine. Eventually, as the negative and addictive effects of cocaine became more well known, it fell out of popularity, and by the beginning of the twentieth century, it was widely outlawed. But not before it had garnered the endorsement of countless writers, politicians, doctors, and, of course, marketers, who promoted the drug into all corners of society.

Although it would be a huge oversimplification to suggest that Angelo Mariani is to blame for the world's ongoing problems with cocaine, it is eye-opening to recognize the degree of influence one relatively unknown man had through a single product, simply because he knew how to leverage the influence of others. Once he convinced prominent thinkers, politicians, and writers that his product was beneficial, they lent him the weight of their own influence.

Degrees of Influence

Today, the idea of an "influencer" has taken on a life of its own, and it is well on its way to becoming a legitimate, if often-mocked, career path. It's not hard to see why. In a digital age when we are bombarded with advertising messages and when the purchase options available for everything from socks to vacation packages can be overwhelming, people want someone they admire or respect to help them make good decisions.

Businesses have realized that in any sector or niche, the endorsement of a person who is known and respected carries more weight with their target market than generic mass marketing, and they are adjusting their allocation of marketing dollars accordingly. For example, there were 1.26 million brand-sponsored Instagram posts in 2016 and an estimated 4.95 million in 2019, meaning there was a nearly 400 percent increase in brand-sponsored social media activity in four years,[3] and the growth rate shows no sign of slowing.

In any group, society, or social structure—including the one you lead—some people have more influence than others. Maybe they've been around for a long time, maybe they have a lot of knowledge, maybe they have strong and loyal relationships, or maybe they are just really good at convincing people. Whatever it is, if you can tap in to that influence, you can multiply your leadership effectiveness. People listen to influencers. What influencers think matters; what they say carries weight; what they endorse or reject sways opinions.

Keep in mind that "influencer" is not a title people bestow upon themselves arbitrarily. There is a difference between a self-proclaimed "influencer" and someone who actually has influence and whose opinion is respected and followed by a large group of people. One of the reasons social media influencers are the butt of so many jokes is because a high number of followers don't always translate into influence. For example, when a young Instagram celebrity with 2.6 million followers tried to launch a clothing line, she couldn't sell even the 36 T-shirts she needed for the initial production run.[4] Although multiple factors may have contributed to the failed product launch, the fact remains that titles, fame, followers, or even success in other areas don't automatically give anyone a platform that translates into effective influence.

True influencers are thought leaders, not just social media celebrities. According to leadership consultant Denise Brosseau of the Thought Leadership Lab, thought leaders are "the informed opinion leaders and the go-to people in their field of expertise."[5] Their influence comes from their power to shape the opinions and decisions of other people in particular areas, and this power is based on things such as expertise in their field, relatability to their audience, and a history of good advice. That last one, history, is one of the most important, because a good track record builds trust equity with followers. True influence can't be faked, forced, or rushed, which is precisely why it's so coveted—and so powerful.

As a leader, it's important for you to identify the true influencers in your team and get them on your side. Doing so is not manipulation—it's respect. These individuals have earned their influence precisely because they take their power seriously, and they won't risk losing it on a whim. If they are hesitant to endorse an idea, you are wise to ask yourself why. Maybe they know something you don't.

Aligning yourself with influencers doesn't mean you surrender your leadership, allow them to block your initiatives, or cave to their whims. It simply means you work to get their buy-in, to win their hearts and loyalty, because they are important players on the team. If you make them upset, you'll make a lot of people upset. If you lose their respect, you'll lose the respect of the people who respect them.

That's the worst-case scenario, though. If you are the right leader for the job, and if the culture of the team is healthy, it's unlikely that you'll find yourself at odds with your influencers. Neither of you is the bad guy, even if you have different opinions, and both of your roles—leader and grassroots influencer—are important.

Who Are Your Influencers?

As a leader, you don't really get to choose who has influence. You might be able to hire or fire or move people around, but just as water naturally finds its level, influencers find their audience. Influence comes in all shapes and sizes: it is not dependent on socioeconomic status, body type, fashion taste, ethnic background, or financial standing. It's an ability some people have, often one they have earned over time, and your goal as a leader is to work with your influencers, not against them. They have their finger on the pulse of the organization. Listen to them, learn from them, win their hearts and trust.

Leadership author Derek Sivers, in his entertaining and effective video "Leadership Lessons from a Dancing Guy," argues that the most important person in any movement is not the leader, but the first follower. In the video, which appears to be taken at a music festival, a shirtless man is seen dancing alone on a hillside, apparently oblivious to anything around him. The people sitting on the grass nearby are watching, a bit confused and clearly hesitant. Then something happens: another man joins the dance. The first dancer welcomes him warmly, and they begin to dance side by side. That is the catalyst. Within seconds, a few more join the dance; and suddenly, people start running to join in. By the end of the three-minute video, the hillside is filled with a crowd dancing, cheering, and applauding. Many of the original doubters have become enthusiastic participants.

Sivers states, "Being a first follower is an under-appreciated form of leadership. The first follower transforms a lone nut into a leader."[6] He adds, "There's no movement without the first follower." The first follower, and probably the second and third, are influencers. The participation of these first followers emboldens people to do something they might have wanted to do (who doesn't want to dance at a music festival?) but didn't feel they had permission to do. Sivers goes on to tell leaders, "Make sure outsiders see more than just the leader. Everyone needs to see the followers, because new followers emulate followers—not the leader." In other words, part of a leader's job is to bring other people into the spotlight.

You are likely to be seen as the "lone nut" in the eyes of some, but when you invite others to join you on stage, not only do you validate them, you allow their support to validate you. Too often, leaders get this backward. We might think that leadership is about people knowing our name, about leading from the front, about the size of our platform or the trust people place in us. Instead, influence often comes down to how many influencers are dancing next to us. Why should we care if people are watching and listening to someone besides us? Only insecure leaders have to be the center of attention all the time. If we are influencing the influencers, we are influencing everyone, regardless of who gets the credit. And the more people we get on board, the sooner we'll reach the tipping point, as Malcolm Gladwell calls it: "that magic moment when an idea, trend, or social behavior crosses a threshold, tips, and spreads like wildfire."[7]

Keep in mind that certain people will respond more quickly to new ideas than others. Everett Rogers's landmark communications theory and book

198

Diffusion of Innovations was first popularized in 1962. The book is now in its fifth edition and, if anything, is more applicable than ever in this age of influencers. Rogers analyzed the process by which people change and adopt innovations, such as new ideas or technology. Based on his research, he identified five categories of people, along with the percentage of the population that falls into each:

> *Innovators* (2.5 percent) are the first people to try anything new. They love risk and adventure.
> *Early adopters* (13.5 percent) are opinion leaders. They are comfortable with new ideas and change, and they take seriously their influence.
> *Early majority* (34 percent) are the first large group to accept new ideas. They don't take the lead, but they don't wait too long to follow, either.
> *Late majority* (34 percent), another large group, tends to resist change. They have a "wait-and-see" mentality and will adopt the new idea only after it's been proven.
> *Laggards* (16 percent) are conservative and very resistant to change; they need to be almost forced to accept new ideas.[8]

If leaders are the innovators in Rogers's model, influencers are the early adopters. Without their buy-in, your ideas and your leadership will have a much harder time influencing the early and late majority. These people aren't hard to convince, though. They already have high risk-tolerance, believe in the power of change, and are smart enough to see the need for it before others do. They are likely to be excited about your ideas once they understand them and see how you are innovating to solve problems.

A mistake that leaders often make is working very hard to convince laggards, who are likely to resist them until the end of time. Instead of investing so much energy in those who are hardwired to resist change, it's more effective to start by convincing the early adopters and early majority. These are your influencers—thought leaders who value both change and leadership, and who already have a following that trusts and listens to them.

In the eyes of the early majority, early adopters can be perceived as more trustworthy than innovators because people may suspect innovators are slightly crazy or out of touch. Innovators are often so far ahead that many people can't relate, or their ideas are seen as risky because they aren't proven. But early adopters are in the middle. They are drawn to new ideas and see their potential, but they are also close enough to the real world for people to trust and follow them.

The pivotal role that early adopters play in connecting innovators and the general public is clearly illustrated in the world of fashion. Every season, designers showcase their latest creations at runway shows, and many of the looks are meant to be editorial, which means they photograph well and get media attention. But often these outfits are so outlandish that "normal" people would never wear them. That's where fashion bloggers and influencers come in: they are fashion-forward enough to identify trends, but they also know how to make those trends relatable, wearable, and therefore buyable for the average person. Fashion designers are the *innovators*; fashion influencers are the *early adopters*; most customers would be the *early* or *late majority*—and you can probably think of a few *laggards* who are still wearing jeans from twenty years ago.

> Often the biggest influencers are not the top leaders, but rather individuals somewhere in the middle.

They don't have the title or the final say, but they have something even more powerful: access and trust. You've probably seen movies where the person pulling the strings in a corporate setting wasn't the CEO, but the receptionist. It is usually played for laughs, but it resonates because there is a lot of truth to it. Influencers in the middle play a key role because they have access upward, to upper management, and downward, to the rank-and-file team member. Their access, combined with earned trust, produces influence.

So what do you do when you need buy-in but your idea faces resistance from those who consider it "out there" or even extreme? Identify your influencers and reach out to them. Explain the why behind the what. Help them process potential questions and reactions so they can then help others who will come along later. Your early adopters are the invisible gatekeepers of influence, and you need their buy-in to reach the people they represent. Your respect for the influence they have earned will go a long way toward getting them to join forces with you.

200

In leadership, you may find yourself in the position of the innovator who introduces change and brings new ideas and new direction to the team. But you don't have to be just a lone nut dancing on a hillside, and you don't have to lead alone. Use your influence to build relationships with your influencers. Share your ideas with people who will care about them and run with them. Influence the influencers, and watch your ideas take off.

KEY TAKEAWAY

Identify the influencers on your team and in your organization and enlist their support to serve and lead people together.

TWENTY-FOUR

Is Anyone Listening?

In the 2019 Open Championship, American golfer Kyle Stanley was widely criticized for not yelling "Fore!" after hitting an errant drive that struck a spectator. Actually, he hit two such balls—and two such spectators—according to his golfing partner, Scottish golfer Robert MacIntyre. The first, on the fourteenth hole, bounced off the leg of a marshal. The second, on the seventeenth hole, hit the mother of MacIntyre's caddie. Thankfully, neither one was injured.

Stanley's mishaps didn't go over well with MacIntyre, who shared what happened next with national Scottish newspaper *The Scotsman*. "Aye, there were harsh words. It wasn't too pleasant. But you've got to tell him it's not right." The problem wasn't that Stanley's drives were off—that happens in golf, as anyone who has ever attempted the game knows all too well. It was that Stanley never shouted the traditional warning. MacIntyre reiterated, "Shout fore. That ball is going straight into the crowd. You know from the word *go* it's going into the crowd. Just shout."[1]

In his defense, Stanley stated that everyone else was yelling the word, so he didn't feel he needed to shout it as well. That wasn't enough to appease his critics in the golfing world, though, because golf etiquette puts the onus on the golfer: "If a player plays a ball in a direction where there is a danger of hitting someone, he should immediately shout a warning. The traditional word of warning in such situations is 'fore.'"[2]

The origin of the term has been lost to history, but there are two primary theories.[3] One is that it is a military term; when a row of soldiers was about to fire, they would shout "Beware before!" to make sure the row in front of them knew to keep their heads ducked. That was eventually shortened to "before" or simply "fore." The second theory, less violent and more plausible, is that the term comes from forecaddies, people who are sometimes stationed down the course to keep an eye on where the ball lands. "Fore!" would have been a logical term for a golfer to yell upon teeing off, mostly as a heads-up to the forecaddie that a ball was on its way—not to save lives but to save golf balls.

If you're on a golf course and you hear a desperate shout of "fore," you don't stop to think. You protect your head and then try to spot the incoming missile before it strikes. It's hard to imagine a more potent, concise, and urgent term in the context of sports. One four-letter word can cause people to dive for cover; usually, those people then yell other four-letter words from the shelter of their golf carts.

As a leader, most of your communication will be longer—and hopefully less desperate—than screaming "fore." But that doesn't mean your communications are any less urgent or any less important.

> *What you say matters, and it should be as clear and concise and effective as possible.*

No offense to Stanley, but in leadership, you can't stand silently by, relying on others to shout your message, and trusting that people will figure out what's coming their way. You have to communicate. You have to make your voice heard and keep your message clear.

Communication is an essential part of leadership. It's how you take something that is in *your* heart, mind, or imagination, and get into *someone else's* heart, mind, or imagination. Successful communication might be the most challenging leadership task you'll face—and also one of the most important. Your effectiveness as a leader is in the degree to which you mobilize your team, which means you have to get really good at communicating to others what is important to you.

We could compare the elements of communication to the process of mailing a gift to someone: you start with the gift in your possession; then you put it in a box and ship it; and finally, your recipient receives, opens, and uses it (or returns it and buys what they really want). This process of sending something from one person to another is analogous to communication, although in the latter case, the "item" being transferred is invisible, and the exchange often takes place instantaneously.

If we break it down, this communication process involves six components: a *sender*, a *recipient*, a *message*, a *code*, a *channel*, and a *response*. Each component is crucial, and, much like the classic children's game of "telephone," each can become dysfunctional or distort the message along the way. Compound that by the multiple people talking and responding and talking again in a leadership context, and you begin to see how important it is for leaders to understand and master each component of the communication process.

1. The Sender: It Starts with You

In team contexts, the communication sender is often you as the leader: you decide to share something you believe could benefit the recipient(s). Your message might convey instructions, values, vision, correction, affirmation, or any number of other things. Maybe it's a memo to the staff about punctuality, for example, or an announcement to the public about an exciting new product or service that is in development, or a conversation with a specific person about an area of work performance that needs improvement.

The message starts with *you*, which means you are responsible for communicating it. You own it, you understand it, and you want to share it. If your communication fails to elicit the desired response, don't be too quick to lay the blame on your recipients. First consider how well you did your part as the sender.

When it comes to communication, leaders tend to focus mostly on their message because they assume the message is all that matters. But the message always comes from a person—you. And you can't separate yourself from your message. In other words, what you communicate will be colored by your worldview, experiences, prejudices, insecurities, goals, and personality. That's inevitable, but inevitability is not an excuse—it's just a

204

reminder to be wise and humble when you communicate. Before you speak, check your motivations, check your attitude, check your facial expressions, and make sure you know what you want to say. Be careful and intentional about what comes out of your mouth or onto your screen.

2. The Recipients: It's All about Them

The recipient of your message might be an individual, a team, an entire organization, customers, church members, volunteers, or any number of others. Regardless, the point of communication is not to launch a message into an unsuspecting universe and hope someone listens. It is to reach a specific audience (whether that's one person or a thousand people) with a specific message. If the audience doesn't get the message, communication failed. Period. That means that reaching the intended recipients is the strategic focus of all communication. In that sense, what you say needs to be more about your recipients than it is about you.

The principle that communication is about the hearers has at least four practical implications. First, *don't get offended if your message is not well received.* For example, if the only people who read your memo about punctuality are the ones who already arrive at work on time, or if your new product announcement is met with yawns instead of cheers, or if the individual you were trying to motivate toward improvement can't seem to understand what the problem is, don't get upset. Take a moment to think about why the reception of your message was less than ideal. If what you say doesn't meet a felt need, or if people don't see the point or understand the relevance of your message, getting mad at them won't help. You might feel sad or frustrated or disappointed, but keep your focus on the people receiving the message, not your feelings. Do your best to improve your messaging, while also remembering that your audience has free will—they determine their own response, and you can't totally control that. Your role as the communication sender is simply to do the best you can to reach your recipients with your message.

Second, *tweak your communication based on feedback from your hearers.* Don't just repeat the same thing louder—find a better way to say it.

That means paying attention to the cues you get from the other party. Whether that party is a person sitting across your desk, a group of people on the receiving end of your email blast, or a roomful of conference attendees, there will usually be some feedback that can help you evaluate and improve your messaging. Maybe it's an email reply, maybe it's the body language of an audience, maybe it's the facial expression of a person you're talking to—these things and many more can give you clues about how well you are getting your message across. Your goal is to communicate, not just to impress, wax eloquent, or vent; so listen to the feedback or read their cues and adjust your communication accordingly.

Third, *pay attention to how well they are paying attention to you.* If your recipients aren't listening, you might as well be addressing an empty room. This is where reading people and reading rooms comes into play. If your hearers are worried, or on their phones, or rushing out the door, or upset with you, or just really tired, don't be in a hurry to get your point across. Good communicators don't jump into the heart of their message until their audience is engaged. That might mean taking a break, telling a joke, asking a question, explaining the problem, changing up your delivery, or simply tabling a discussion until a better time.

And finally, *know your audience.* The better you understand your audience, the better you'll know how to speak to them. What are they worried about? What do they care about? What do they want to accomplish? What approach or presentation or wording or illustration will help *them* the most? Leadership is about serving people, and communication is an important tool you can use to better serve your team.

3. The Message: What You Want to Say

"First learn the meaning of what you say, and then speak," taught the ancient Greek philosopher Epictetus.[4] In other words, think before you speak, as your parents tried to tell you when you were growing up. You know the essence of what you want to say, but the hard work is what comes next, and it needs to happen before you call a staff meeting or fire off a group text message. Identify exactly what you feel, believe, and want. You need to offer more than a vague idea if you want to reach people's minds and hearts. Work through your thoughts on your own first. Sort out the pros and cons, the risks and advantages. Break your message down into distinct parts and ensure each one makes sense. There is a place for processing ideas out loud and off the top of your head, but if you're planning to do that, give people fair warning that you're processing, not proclaiming, and don't frame mental or emotional musings as decisions or facts.

4. The Code: Language Matters

How does your message cross from your mind to the mind of the recipient? It must be encoded in written or spoken words, body language, pictures, charts, tables, mottoes, lists, or anything else that expresses your message. In the shipping analogy, the message is the gift, and the code is the box that carries it to the recipient. Messages don't telepathically appear in someone else's brain: they must be translated into a shared code that conveys your meaning.

That's all language is, actually: a communication code. We laugh when we see people who speak different languages trying to communicate by talking more loudly or slowly, as if the problem were somehow with the other person's hearing. But the problem isn't lack of hearing; it's lack of a shared code, the language used to transmit a message. Similar problems can occur when leaders fail to communicate in terms their recipients can fully understand, even when they do in fact share the same language. This might happen for any number of reasons: your email was rushed and too confusing; you showed up to a meeting stressed and came across too aggressive; your graphs were too complicated; or you simply didn't have the words to explain what you meant when you answered a question. All of them are code fails.

Your job isn't done just because you spoke your mind in whatever form suited you in the moment. You have to make sure your message was properly deciphered on arrival. That's on you as the sender more than the recipient, and it comes back to knowing your audience well.

How can you do that? One way is to *speak in the same language as the hearer.* I don't mean a literal language like English or Spanish or Chinese, of course (that's a given), but a metaphorical language, the "code" I mentioned above. In other words, use words, illustrations, logic, and humor that will be understood by your hearers.

Second, *communicate empathetically*. That is, put yourself in the recipients' shoes for a minute. Do your best to understand how they will interpret what you are saying on both an informational and emotional level. That's not easy, which is precisely why communication is a skill—you have to learn how to say things in a way that people will understand. For example, before sending an important email, reread the entire thing, thinking about what the recipients will read and feel, and making sure you are communicating both the information and the emotion you intend.

Finally, *make sure your verbal and nonverbal communication are aligned*. In other words, consider how your body language, tone, and approach will be received and whether they support or contradict your words. Do you sound like you're joking when you're actually serious? Do you look angry but you're just deep in thought? Do you seem disinterested when you're really processing ideas? You may need to remind your face to reflect your thoughts and your words.

5. The Channel: Reaching Crowds, Not Crickets

If, for the sake of nostalgia, you've ever logged in to an old social media account (such as your MySpace account from 2008) and posted something, and then received absolutely no response because your friends abandoned that channel years ago, you know what an ineffective communication channel is. It is any channel your target audience isn't using. You can send out eloquent messages all you want, but if no one is tuned in to that channel, you're not communicating.

As a leader, utilize the means of communication best suited to reach your target audience, whether that is a person, your team, or the public at large. Before you default to the channel you are most comfortable with or have traditionally used, identify the channel your audience is listening to most and the one that will best communicate your message. You might use email, texts, social media posts, sticky notes, to-do lists, hallway meetings, weekly staff meetings, one-on-one conversations, video conferences, project management software, or any other of the myriad of communication options that exist or will exist in the future. The point is, find what works.

Communication is never easy or perfect, so you'll continually be looking for ways to send out your message more effectively. It helps to diversify across multiple channels, because different audiences tend to gravitate toward different platforms or strategies. As a leader, you will likely have to choose a master communication strategy for work purposes, such as getting everybody onboard with a particular app or software; but that doesn't eliminate the need for being smart about messaging across other channels as well.

6. The Response: Communicate for Change

In his book *Communicating for a Change,* communicator and pastor Andy Stanley recommends "refusing to stand up and speak until you know the answer to two questions: What is the one thing I want my audience to know? What do I want them to do about it?"[5] Your goal in communication is generally to both convey information and to persuade, because you are a leader and you want to take people in a certain direction. You aren't just transmitting data randomly; you're using it to make a point. You're motivating and guiding people toward a goal. So most communication is intended to produce some sort of response. You need to know what response you are looking for before you communicate in order to measure the success of the messaging.

The response of the recipient indicates the effectiveness of the communication. Even if the response is not what you were hoping for, it at least tells you the extent to which your message was received. Are your recipients confused or informed? Excited or scared? Encouraged or frustrated?

People make decisions based on their understanding, which consists primarily of their mental and emotional perception of what is true. If you can help them understand your message, they will likely respond in the way you hoped they would. If you can't, you'll be fighting an uphill battle, trying to override their logical and emotional barriers. Understanding is key, and it's worth taking the time to help people grasp what you are saying and why it is important and true.

Based on the response, you can decide how to continue. Assuming the message was received and internalized, you can expect it to be acted upon. If you can tell the message wasn't received the right way, or wasn't received at all, don't repeat it ad nauseum. Go back to the steps above. Make sure you and the recipient are on the same page, and that it's the right page. Think through your message again and make it even clearer. Evaluate the way you are communicating (the code) and the channel through which you are sending the message.

You might need to do additional homework, ask more questions, reach out to some influencers, or simply wait for a better time. But whatever you do, don't just settle for watching golf balls fly toward crowds, hoping someone else speaks up. Your team and your objectives are too important to leave communication to chance.

KEY TAKEAWAY

Communication is more than just talking at people: it is understanding your hearers, reaching them effectively with your message, and obtaining results.

TWENTY-FIVE

Meetings Matter

Meetings. If there is one aspect of team leadership and organizational life that seems to be universally hated, it's meetings. Everyone from employees to managers to volunteers to CEOs complains about them, but meetings seem to be a necessary evil and so we keep scheduling them. Patrick Lencioni, business consultant and author of the book *Death by Meeting*, states, "We have come to accept that the activity most central to the running of our organizations is inherently painful and unproductive."[1]

The two reasons most people cite for dreading meetings are that there are way too many of them, and they aren't very effective. Research on meetings seems to bear that out. Elise Keith, cofounder of software firm Lucid Meetings, has done extensive research on the number, size, and effectiveness of meetings in the business world. She estimates there are between 36 million and 54 million meetings held *every day* in the United States alone. She also estimates ineffective meetings could be costing the US economy $70 billion to $283 billion a year, depending on the definition of an ineffective meeting.[2] Even the low end of that range is a staggering amount of waste.

A recent study cited in *Harvard Business Review* analyzed the Outlook calendars of everyone in a large organization, looking for information about how much time they spent in meetings in a year. In particular, they wanted to look at the ripple effect of the weekly executive committee meeting. They found that company-wide, between the executive meeting and the meetings required to support it, company employees spent a collective three hundred thousand hours each year in meetings. That didn't even include the time spent gathering information for those meetings or time spent in other, unrelated meetings.[3]

And yet, meetings are vital to organizational life; and they certainly aren't all bad, not by a long shot. Lencioni states, "There is simply no substitute for a good meeting—a dynamic, passionate, and focused engagement—when it comes to extracting the collective wisdom of a team."[4] If you've been in a great meeting, you know the power that flows from conversation and collaboration around a specific goal. You walk away from that kind of meeting energized and enthusiastic, simultaneously dreaming of the future and planning your next steps. You know your role and the roles of others better than ever. You feel connected to the team's overall vision and you feel integral to reaching that vision.

The problem is, many of us don't know how to lead a good meeting, much less a great one. At worst, our meetings are long, disorganized, boring, and ineffective. They start late and end even later. They cover a bewildering range of topics without making solid decisions on most. This is the opposite of what we intend, of course, but unless we are intentional about running meetings, they will run us, and we won't like the results.

Five Characteristics of a Great Meeting

What does a great meeting look like? It depends a great deal on your organization, your team, your personality, and the needs of the season, so you'll need to experiment and tweak things until you find what works. But to get you started, here are a few goals to aim for.

1. A Great Meeting Has a Focused Agenda

A focused meeting has an agenda that is planned in advance, and it sticks to the agenda. To quote Lencioni again: "The single biggest structural problem facing leaders of meetings is the tendency to throw every type of issue that needs to be discussed into the same meeting, like a bad stew with too many random ingredients."[5]

Good meetings have a reason to exist, and everyone present knows what that is. People arrive prepared, feel ownership in the issues, engage in constructive dialogue, and leave with action items to focus on. Good meetings also have a start and end time. If you find yourself going off-topic or spending too much time on each topic, estimate in advance how much time each topic should be allotted and set a timer. When the timer goes off, make a decision about the issue and move on.

There is a limit to how many items can be addressed in one setting, and that limit isn't set by the leader's agenda. It's set by the brain, and it's called decision fatigue. Social psychologist Roy Baumeister has analyzed decision-making in depth. In his rather darkly titled paper, "The Psychology of Irrationality: Why People Make Foolish, Self-Defeating Choices," he shows that humans tend to make self-defeating choices when forced to make too many decisions at once. He writes:

> Making choices is hard work that depletes an inner resource that seems quite limited. People can only really make a few serious choices at a time, and then the capacity for choosing has to recover and replenish before they are fully effective again.[6]

That's not to say you'll never follow a rabbit trail in a meeting, but it should be the exception. Rabbit trails usually just lead to more rabbit trails, and often rabbit droppings, but rarely to actual rabbits; and while it can be interesting to occasionally go off-topic, sometimes it's just an excuse to avoid the decisions at hand. Not only do you lose time and get distracted from what matters, you deplete the limited mental energy needed for decision-making. When you finally do get to the agenda items, the team is tired and ready to go home, leading to rushed decisions or tabled discussions.

People's time is valuable, and they know when it is being wasted in discussions that should have been emails or one-on-one conversations. It's far more productive to keep the meeting focused, even if that means leaving a few rabbits unchased. Once your meetings get a reputation for getting things done, people will be more likely to be prepared for them, on time for them, and even excited about them, because they will know their time is being respected and utilized well.

2. A Great Meeting Gets the Right People around the Table

To increase the efficiency of work teams and meetings, Jeff Bezos, multibillionaire founder and owner of Amazon.com, instituted a simple, company-wide rule known as the "two-pizza team." He insisted that every team should be small enough to be fed with two pizzas.[7] That doesn't mean teams actually eat pizza at every meeting, but the policy is an effective one for keeping meetings small, efficient, and focused.

If you can get all the right people (and hopefully only the right people) to the table, and if you have a focused agenda, your meeting has a much higher chance of being infused with energy from the start. When the right people tackle issues together, creativity sparks creativity; ideas play off each other and complement each other; problems are met with solutions rather than panic; ideas are debated and curated, discarded or improved. It's teamwork at its best, and the result is collaborative genius.

Who are "the right people"? You're the leader, so you probably have a sense of that already, but here are a few things to look for.

- People who are *knowledgeable*. You need facts, not guesses, so get the experts into the room and let them inform everyone else.
- People who are *empowered*. Team members need authority to make changes, so invite people who are positioned to carry out team decisions.
- People who are *different*. That is, people who are different from you and different from each other, who represent a variety of worldviews, ethnic backgrounds, beliefs, genders, and more. Diversity is your friend because every unique viewpoint represents a sector of society you may never fully understand; value diversity and be intentional about nurturing it.
- People who are *sharp*. "Sharp" is hard to quantify, but it refers to someone who is both smart and quick thinking; someone who knows

214

a lot, but who also knows how to apply what they know to real-life situations. It's more than knowledge, intelligence, formal education, or street smarts, although ideally it includes them. You need sharp people around you, because you'll bring out the best in each other.

- People who are *creative*. Problem solving is what creative people do best; they see thing differently than you or someone else might see them, and they can spot solutions in places other people would never look.

- People who are *invested*. People around your decision-making table need to care about the organization and be motivated to work toward solutions, rather than being apathetic or half-hearted.

- People who are *secure*. The first idea or solution is rarely the best idea, but it might be the starting place for the best idea. Secure people have thick enough skin to debate ideas productively.

Getting the right people to the right tables is not easy, but it's worth pursuing. Notice I said *tables*, plural. You'll face many decisions in many areas, so you'll probably have multiple decision-making meetings. Take time to think through who is best equipped to make the right decisions in each meeting.

3. A Great Meeting Is Collaborative

If you have the right people around the table, let them talk. Don't dominate the conversation, and don't let anyone else dominate, either. As a rule of thumb, any meeting in which one person does all the talking should have been an email. There are coffee mugs out there that say that. Buy one.

By definition, collaboration refers to people with different talents and viewpoints working together. When that happens, sparks often fly—in a good way. Heated discussions likely mean you have *diverse opinions* and *people who care*, both of which are positives. People should behave like mature adults in those discussions, of course, but that doesn't mean they'll always get along. Don't be afraid of emotion or strong opinions. Invite

215

authentic discussion. Honest disagreement and debate might be exactly what your meetings need. They break topics open and bring issues to the surface like nothing else.

4. A Great Meeting Results in Decisions

Most meetings are for decision-making rather than brainstorming. A roomful of people means a roomful of opinions, so you could analyze and debate an idea forever without reaching absolute consensus. Allow time for a good discussion, but at some point, make a decision. Then write it down, assign responsibilities with due dates, and set follow-up dates. Decisions create momentum, and meetings run better with momentum.

Both leadership and meetings are less about massive changes and more about constant course correction. There are few things scarier than to be on an airplane and experience a sudden and dramatic change in altitude or direction. To avoid that scenario, pilots make frequent minor course adjustments as needed to stay on course, and most passengers barely notice. Making small, timely course corrections as you go along helps eliminate the last-second 180-degree turns that create panic and have people diving for their oxygen masks. This is why regular meetings are so valuable, because they enable you to keep track of the current state of the organization and to make adjustments as needed.

5. A Great Meeting Gives Life

This may be the hardest one to believe if you're used to walking out of meetings frustrated and deflated, but maybe you need to change the way you view those meetings. The goal of meetings is the good of the team and the organization, which is a positive. Meetings might sometimes include some bad news and a few mind-numbing reports, but ultimately, they are about life, growth, and progress toward goals. Keep your focus on the purpose of the meetings, and make sure the meetings you lead are infused with hope and positivity.

If a meeting is boring, change it up. After all, it's your meeting, and you are the leader. Order those two pizzas if you need to. Be fresh, be creative, be innovative, be human. I regularly change the order of our staff meetings if they start to feel stale. The elements of the meeting are usually the same—recapping wins, giving out needed information, an inspirational message, announcements, and so on—but the order will change, or I'll throw in some shout-outs, or I'll give out awards or a gift card, or I'll stage a random competition or game. Humor helps a lot, too, especially when it's self-deprecating. Laughter and meetings don't have to be mutually exclusive. Well-used humor doesn't undermine the seriousness of the topic at hand; rather, it helps people and leaders alike stay in touch with their humanity, which is grounding and refreshing for everyone.

"Great meeting" doesn't have to be an oxymoron—you can hold efficient, effective, energized meetings with a little bit of planning and self-discipline. A focused agenda, the right people, a collaborative process, a focus on decision-making, and an inspiring, life-giving environment will all contribute to making your meetings some of the most productive moments of your week.

ooo

Learn to love meetings, because meetings matter. Like a football huddle, they are an essential part of getting individual players to run the same play. And when that happens, the energy is obvious. You can feel it, the team can feel it, your clients or customers or church can feel it. Focused, effective meetings capture the essence of teamwork: getting things done together.

> **KEY TAKEAWAY**
>
> Meetings matter because they bring teams together to accomplish common goals, so be intentional and creative about leading effective meetings.

TWENTY-SIX

Work Your Systems

William Edwards Deming was an obscure Wyoming statistician in 1950 when his research on quality control came to the attention of Japanese industrial leaders. Japan was reeling from the effects of World War II, struggling to rebuild a shattered economy, and eager to participate in world markets. Deming was invited to give a series of lectures in Japan on his quality-control principles, and his message was quickly embraced. Applying his methods produced such enormous success that the Japanese created the Deming Prize for companies that made notable advances in quality, which quickly became one of the awards most sought after by Japanese companies.[1]

Meanwhile, in the United States, the pursuit of quality was seen as expensive and secondary. That is, until Japanese brands such as Sony and Panasonic began to decimate the American consumer-electronics industry, and reliable, fuel-efficient Toyotas and Hondas made deep inroads in the American automobile industry, affecting automakers like Ford and General Motors. In 1980, NBC aired a documentary titled, *If Japan Can, Why Can't We?* The broadcast spotlighted Japan's manufacturing prowess in comparison to American corporations, and also mentioned the role of Deming, who was almost unknown at the time in his own country. Soon after, however, Deming became one of the most-sought-after corporate consultants in the nation.[2]

Ford Motor Company, one of the first large American corporations to seek Deming's help, asked him to visit their Michigan headquarters in February 1981. The company's sales were faltering, and it was hemorrhaging cash—to the tune of $3 billion between 1979–1982.[3] When Deming arrived, executives were expecting a crash course in quality, states business journalist John Holusha in the *New York Times*. Instead, he started asking questions about the company's culture, management, and commitment to constancy. He understood that Ford needed more than a superficial program: it needed a philosophical and systemic overhaul. Ford applied Deming's principles over the next few years, and the results were dramatic. By 1986, Ford had become the most profitable auto company in the United States.[4]

Deming was well-known for his bluntness. Holusha says that he "spoke to senior executives as if they were schoolboys" and "delighted in telling corporate chieftains . . . that they were a significant part of the problem." His theories were founded on the premise that most product defects result from systems and management issues rather than careless workers. Therefore, his focus was on designing efficient processes that would produce quality from the start, rather than producing quantity and inspecting for quality after the fact, which was the prevailing management method. He said management based mainly on evaluating results is "like driving a car by looking in the rearview mirror," and that if quality inspection theory were "applied to making toast [it] would be expressed: 'You burn, I'll scrape.'"[5]

Deming advocated thinking about systems proactively, and he created a quality control process he called the PDSA Cycle (Plan-Do-Study-Act):[6] create a plan, carry it out, analyze the results, and make needed adjustments. Then the cycle repeats, with continual adjustments being made until the process is as efficient as possible. As a statistician, he advocated using statistics to detect flaws in production processes, but he also developed a broad management philosophy that emphasized problem solving based on treating workers as collaborators and empowering them to work with excellence by giving them the freedom, tools, systems, and support they needed to do their best work.

Deming's groundbreaking theories changed the landscape of corporate America and were foundational to Six Sigma and other quality-control plans that are common today. Holusha quotes John O. Whitney, a renowned turnaround expert, as saying, "Today CEOs understand the importance of process because of Deming. This has been a sea change in American business."

Good Results Start with Good Systems

Deming's goal was quality, but his focus was systems. He understood that healthy systems and processes are essential to quality, and quality is essential to ongoing success. Quality control is simply making sure your product or service is excellent, that it meets or exceeds expectations. Leaders who care about ongoing quality must care about systems, therefore, because healthy systems are the key to maintaining excellence over an extended period of time.

An organizational system refers to a set of established procedures to get something done. In other words, your *organization* must be *organized*. That seems like it should go without saying, but it doesn't. You need plans, processes, and procedures. Too often, leaders want to ad hoc their way through life and business, making things up as they go along. As a leader, you can fly by the seat of your pants only for so long before you crash into a mountain in the fog. If you want results that are scalable, sustainable, and reproducible, you have to have good systems.

Systems are the best friend of vision.

Creating systems is part of the hard work of leadership, which is why leaders sometimes never get around to it. It's more fun to cast vision and create strategies. It's exciting to brainstorm, to fill whiteboards with ideas you hope to carry out. But there is only one way to turn the whiteboards into reality: by creating robust systems.

Some leaders think structure will cramp their style and limit their dreams, but the opposite is almost always true. Systems provide the infrastructure that gives strength to your dreams. You can visualize and strategize all you want, but unless you have solid systems, it will be difficult, maybe impossible, to bring those dreams to pass, because you'll waste time, effort, and money on activities that should have been automated and standardized.

Accounting systems, for example, make sure the money you earn isn't lost or misplaced. Budgeting systems help you use money wisely and plan for the future. Hiring systems increase your ability to screen and hire the best people. You might have systems to plan and run live events, to produce videos, to coordinate book tours, to launch new products, to run your social media accounts, to track inventory, and so on. Systems help make dreams tangible by giving you and your team objective steps to take day in and day out as you pursue the future you envision.

On the other hand, if structure is resisted and ambiguity is tolerated, mediocrity is inevitable. You can't create an organizational culture that disdains order and still expect anything you build to last. Disorder and excellence are, sooner or later, mutually exclusive. Of course, there will be seasons of change and growth in any organization, and that can bring some chaos. But chaos should never be a lifestyle, or worse yet, a value. Leaders should strive to bring order from disorder and direction out of ambiguity—and that's what good systems do.

People Problems Are Usually Systems Problems

Dr. Paul Batalden, author and healthcare quality guru, observed, "Every system is perfectly designed to get the results it gets."[7] In other words, your current reality is a result of your systems. If you don't like the results you're getting, the first place to look is the system—not the people—that produced the results. As Deming pointed out, most problems (and therefore the most potential for improvement) lie with management and systems, not with the people downline. When there's a chronic problem, we tend to blame it on the ineptitude of others, or even attribute it to our own poor leadership. However, in many cases, neither of those is the primary issue: the issue is a problem with our systems. Yet another Deming quote: "Quality is made in the boardroom. A worker can deliver lower quality, but she cannot deliver quality better than the system allows."[8]

Our church rents meeting space every Sunday morning at a local school, and every week we set up early, hold our services, and tear down in the afternoon. I thought things were going smoothly until the school administrator recently informed me that our team was loading out thirty minutes late every week. I was appalled—but not at any one person or even at the lack of a load-out system. What appalled me was the fact that we didn't have a *reporting* system to alert our leadership team there was an issue in the first place. That's not the responsibility of people at the bottom of our team's authority structure—it's mine. I have to make sure systems are in place to facilitate and standardize what we are doing, and to alert us to problems long before a landlord has to complain.

In general, fix systems before you fire people. Yes, people's mistakes and misbehavior need to be dealt with. But it's surprising how often errors, behavioral issues, strange decisions, or attitude problems are only symptoms of deeper systemic problems. For example, maybe they were asked to meet a certain quota but don't have the tools to do so; or they were tasked with making a project happen but not given the authority or the personnel they needed; or they are reporting to multiple supervisors who contradict one another, and they are caught in the middle. No one can thrive in an environment where the systems that should help them instead oppose them, and you can't blame people for mistakes or strong emotions that are the result of broken systems. Fix the systemic problem and you'll likely fix the person; fire the person and you might experience a temporary improvement, but if the problem isn't fixed, the next person in that role might well develop the same issues.

Five Benefits of Systems

While most leaders would agree systems are important, at least in theory, systems are not easy to implement, and they are often overlooked in the rush to get projects done, deals closed, meetings organized. Creating systems is one of those important tasks that often fall victim to the tyranny of the urgent. While creating systems is one of the hardest parts of leadership, it will ultimately make life easier for everyone. Here are five benefits you can expect when you make systems a priority.

1. Systems Promote Efficiency

Not having a system is also a system. If you don't have established processes in your organization or team, then you have a default system, and usually that system is *you*. You have to answer questions. You have to dole out petty cash. You have to authorize spending. You have to approve vacations. You have to book travel. You have to drive across town at 3:00 a.m. to see why the office alarm is going off. These default systems are not healthy or sustainable, and they are certainly not efficient.

When you create systems, you eliminate the need to make the same decision over and over. That's the thought process behind the limited wardrobes of leaders such as Barack Obama, Mark Zuckerberg, and Steve Jobs—it helps reduce decision fatigue.[9] I enjoy fashion too much to follow their lead on that one, but I appreciate the focus on eliminating unnecessary decisions, which is exactly what established procedures and protocol do.

2. Systems Assign Clear Roles and Responsibilities

If you've ever seen two baseball outfielders collide while chasing a fly ball, you know what a system breakdown looks like: chaos, collisions, and missed opportunities. Most people respond to ambiguity (which is the opposite of clear systems) by trying to do everything, by doing nothing, or by doing only what they feel like doing. If your whole team is in that mode, you will have chaos and waste—and fumbled fly balls. Systems help eliminate duplicated efforts or dropped responsibilities by clearly defining roles and responsibilities.

3. Systems Provide Protection

Accounting systems can keep you out of bankruptcy—or jail. Sexual harassment policies, hiring and firing procedures, standards for setting salaries, and so on are all systems that protect you and your team. Clear systems also help prevent relational breakdown, frustration, and offense by providing clear expectations and promoting fair, consistent treatment of people.

4. Systems Help Onboard New Team Members

When teams are small, bringing in a new team member isn't difficult. But over time, especially as leaders at the top of the org chart have less involvement with certain sectors of the organization, new team members won't have the benefit of learning directly from those leaders. New hires need roles, systems, and processes that are clearly defined so they can hit the ground running, rather than slowing up everyone around them while they try to get up to speed.

5. Systems Build Success

Systems come *before* success. Too often, leaders treat systems as an afterthought, something to put into place after things are working smoothly so they can go on vacation once in a while and not have the place burn down or blow up while they're gone. But the best systems don't just standardize what has worked so far—they prepare the team to reach the next goal. Systems link the present with the future. The best systems move a team forward, rather than tie it to the past.

These are just five of the many benefits of implementing systems in your leadership, with your team, and throughout your organization. That brings up the next logical question, though: how do we create and sustain good systems?

Building Great Systems

One of the best strategies to create systems is deceptively simple: *build as you go*. If something complicated, negative, or challenging happens and you have to deal with it, ask yourself if the issue is reasonably likely to happen again. If so, decide how you're going to handle it now. Start a system. Then, as needed and over time, tweak the system. I mentioned above the lack of a reporting system for our load-out procedure—that was an easy one to fix. We established a simple reporting system. A specific team member is now in charge of noting the load-out time each week and reporting it to the person who compiles our Monday Report. As a result of that simple change, we have a weekly data point that helps us stay accountable to our rental agreement.

A second strategy to build great systems is to *ask for help*. You don't have to do this alone. If you aren't naturally gifted at organization—or if you are gifted but you just don't have time to create a needed system—look for people on your team who are better equipped or positioned to create the system. There is probably a person on your team who has already noticed the problem and would love to help solve it, if you would just ask. Also, ask for help from the people on the ground, those who are closest to the issue you are trying to address, rather than imposing decisions from a distance. Get their feedback and opinions before you make drastic changes. And of course, you can get help by learning from other organizations that are doing what you want to do.

Take advantage of the information and personnel you have around you.

Third, *continually improve your systems.* Once you've created a system, it will need frequent tinkering to keep it efficient and effective. The good news is that systems are usually much easier to fix than to start. That's the genius of Deming's whole Plan-Do-Study-Act methodology: each time you study your system's results, make the indicated changes, and try your system again, you improve your system—and the quality and effectiveness of your work.

You don't have to have all the answers and build all the systems, all the time, all on your own.

In my experience, this need for tinkering usually happens just when you feel your systems are in place, all the responsibilities are delegated, and all the job descriptions are written. That's when something—or everything—changes and you have to make adjustments. Get used to it. Tweaking systems is a part of growth. Your obsession must be improvement, and better systems are a key to improving just about everything.

Finally, to build great systems, *make systems work for you,* not the other way around. It's your system, and it's meant to serve you and your team, not control you. Don't let systems take on a life of their own or become an end in themselves. For example, if your organization has traditionally held an annual event for stakeholders, but now the event seems to take more work than it's worth, and you are getting the feeling you have to beg people to attend anyway, consider canceling the event. At one time, the event served a need, and therefore it was valuable; but if the event is no longer meeting the need, or if the need itself no longer exists, then the event

225

has lost its value. Systems shouldn't become sacred cows. When they no longer serve your purpose, change them or eliminate them, but don't start serving them. As a leader, you need to walk the fine line between creating order and moving forward. If you remember that systems point toward the future, you'll be able to navigate growth and change wisely, working your systems rather than letting them work you.

ooo

Love people and love your vision, but also love systems. They are the key to serving those people and achieving that vision. Once you learn to make systems work for you, you'll never go back, because the right system will always take your leadership and your team to the next level.

KEY TAKEAWAY

By providing structure and sustainability, healthy systems build your organization, serve your team, and help you achieve your vision.

TWENTY-SEVEN

Known and Needed

In the highly competitive world of college football recruiting, coaches will do just about anything to sign top prospects. That includes showing up to high school games in helicopters to impress potential recruits, creating custom comic books or fake *Sports Illustrated* covers starring the players they are courting, and just about any other stunt you can think of.[1] And it's not just high school players being scouted, either. In California, a ten-year-old was reportedly offered a scholarship by more than one college—despite the fact he couldn't sign a letter of intent for ten more years.[2] Many of the crazier tactics coaches have tried have subsequently been outlawed by the National Collegiate Athletic Association (NCAA), but that doesn't keep recruiters from looking for loopholes and new tactics to encourage recruitment. Coaches are always aware of who is about to leave the team and who could potentially join, which is why they invest so much research, money, and effort into the recruitment process.

Creative recruiting tactics may get a lot of attention, but I recently watched a sports channel interview that demonstrated a tactic that was even more effective. The interview was with one of the top high school players in the nation, a young man who had just announced his college choice. He was accompanied by his father and the coach of the team he had chosen. After the young man finished, the coach stepped up to the mic and began talking about the qualities, character, and talents of the new recruit. The coach clearly had a knowledge not just of the player's stats, but an understanding of who he was as a person and how he would flourish on his new team. Once the coach was done, the young man's father said, "And that is why my son chose this school. The coach knows him so well, he described him better than I could have myself."

The coach was Dabo Swinney of Clemson University in South Carolina. Swinney has become a recruiting legend. *Sports Illustrated* called the program Swinney created "the pre-eminent recruiting program in America."[3] I believe the key to Swinney's success was revealed in the comment from the young man's father: not tricks, stunts, or loopholes, but genuinely knowing his players and making them feel needed on the team.

As Dabo Swinney's recruitment strategy illustrates, a key to attracting the right people is to help them feel *known* and *needed*. We will look at those two things in more detail below, but first, it's important to recognize why recruiting is so important for leaders.

Leaders Are Recruiters

Just as football coaches are in constant recruitment mode, leaders must always be recruiting the best talent for their team and organization. In business, that means attracting highly qualified employees to fill key positions as well as building out effective teams throughout the company. In churches and other nonprofit organizations, it means motivating people to volunteer their time and talents. You need to be in constant recruitment mode for two reasons: *turnover* and *growth*.

Turnover: People Come and People Go

Turnover is a natural part of any organization. Teams are made of people, and people change, grow, get bored, get mad, get sick, go back to school, move away, have kids, start their own business, take other jobs, retire, and any other number of things that can affect their involvement in your team. Remember, you don't control people: you serve people. If you truly love those you lead, you'll want the best for them, which might mean letting them go.

Letting them go is not easy if you've worked together heart and soul—if you've invested in them, loved them, mentored them, and come to depend on them—only to have them move on. But you have to be okay with that. On the flipside, you will also be able to receive the benefit of hiring people who were mentored and trained by others. This coming and going is the organizational equivalent of cross-pollination in the plant world: organizations are strengthened by the ideas and experiences people bring with them from organizations they served before.

No one is dispensable, but everyone can be replaced. Instead of panicking when a key person leaves, view it as a chance to rethink roles and systems. Changing up roles is often a positive step because it jump-starts healthy reorganization. Keep a positive outlook: choose to believe the perfect person for the job is about to submit a résumé, and you will continue to move forward as a team.

When people leave, be grateful for the contributions and investments they made. Your organization is better because they were there. Gratitude goes a long way toward smoothing over transitions. Plus, if you keep the transition positive, they may end up returning to your organization down the road.

Whenever possible, look first within your own ranks to fill the role because current team members already have knowledge and relationships that will ease the transition. But don't lock yourself into that either, since talent can come from anywhere.

Growth: You'll Never Outgrow Your Team

Your team defines your reach and your effectiveness, both as a leader and as an organization. The organization might begin to grow beyond what your team is able to handle, but if you don't quickly adjust and expand, your growth will slow or stop until you build a team capable of sustaining continued growth.

Jim Collins is a business management expert and author of the bestselling book *Good to Great: Why Some Companies Make the Leap . . . and Others Don't*. He and his teams studied a wide array of companies and leaders to determine what qualities carried companies to greatness. He writes, "Those who build great companies understand that the ultimate throttle on growth for any great company is not markets, or technology, or competition, or products. It is one thing above all others: the ability to get and keep enough of the right people."[4]

> *The effectiveness of any team, business, or organization is directly correlated to the people and the systems that run it.*

If you want to grow your organization, you need to continually be recruiting new talent. You might not know exactly how people will fit in or what they'll do, but if you identify the right people for your team, you'll have access to the human resources you need to build better teams and a better future. Collins calls this getting the right people on the bus:

> We expected that good-to-great leaders would begin by setting a new vision and strategy. We found instead that they first got the right people on the bus, the wrong people off the bus, and the right people in the right seats—and then they figured out where to drive it.[5]

That means one of your primary tasks as a leader is not to set vision but to gather and guide people. Vision is vital, as we saw earlier, but people are the first and most important component of leadership. Never assume you have a big enough team; never lose the capacity to befriend and believe in new people; and never grow so enamored with where you are going that you overlook the team that is taking you there.

Known and Needed

How do you recruit the right people? The first step is what we discussed earlier: by becoming followable. If you learn to lead yourself—if you become the leader you would want to follow—then others will follow you too. That doesn't mean they will appear out of thin air, though. Often the best talent won't come to you. They'll wait for you to find them, to invite them, to encourage them, to show them they are known and needed.

Known

Everyone wants to be known, even the most introverted among us. To be known is to be recognized and to be valued. To be known helps us feel like we are more than a number or a face in a crowd: we are individuals with recognized strengths, characteristics, and contributions.

As a leader, don't just spend time with your immediate team. Look two or three circles past your inner circle. Get to know the up-and-coming leaders, the young people rising through the ranks, the newcomers who are just getting settled, the quiet people who rarely make a splash but are always there, the loud people others might write off as immature. Find the geniuses and the creatives, the warriors and the marathoners. Make it your goal to know as many people as possible, both within your organization and outside it, because people need to believe that they are known and that they matter.

You can't fake genuine interest, but you shouldn't need to if you care about people. Sometimes the craziness of leadership and the weird dynamics of power and fame can combine to isolate leaders, and you need to fight against that. Never forget the early days, when you were happy to have *anyone* follow you or work alongside you, even if they had a few quirks. If you find yourself increasingly isolated—in your office, your boardroom, or your greenroom—get out for a while. Go meet someone new. Show genuine interest in people who might never imagine you knew they existed. Ask people what they enjoy about their job; ask about their family, about their dreams, about their needs. This is one of the most refreshing things you can do as a leader because it reminds you why you do what you do (it's for people) and how you got where you are (it was with people).

Needed

Not only do people need to be known, they need to be needed. They need to see that their contribution matters, that they are making a difference. They need to feel that their role is part of something bigger and that the future will be better because of the part they are playing now.

One of the simplest ways to help people feel needed is to *express gratitude*. Say thank you—a lot. As a leader, your gratitude affirms not just the value of what was done but the significance of the people who did it. Gratitude says, "I see you, I recognize you, and I depend on you. You are needed." That's more than good manners, which we mentioned earlier; it's also an acknowledgment: "I am not a lone ranger. I couldn't do what I do without your contribution. What you do is integral to the success of the team."

Another effective way to help people feel needed is to *ask for help*. Even if people are volunteers, they are there because they want to make a difference. Whether staff or volunteers, people tend to rise to the level of the needs set before them and the expectations placed upon them. If they've bought into the vision of the team or organization, they will usually be happy to help.

When we first launched our church in Los Angeles, I met a young couple one Sunday after services had ended. They told me that they were from Australia but were living in L.A., and that in Australia they had attended Hillsong Church. I was intrigued. Maybe their experience and background could help us with our fledgling church plant. I invited them to a party we were hosting at my house that night and introduced them to a few people. That same night, I asked if they would be interested in volunteering with us in a minor capacity as we got to know each other better. They quickly became very involved in our church community and were a huge asset, and one of them eventually came on staff and worked with us for three years. I wonder what would have happened if, that first day after church, I would have just said, "It's so nice to meet you, I hope you feel welcome here."

Being known and being needed are connected.

That's not wrong, of course—but people need to be needed. What attracted that couple to our team was the fact that there was a place for them to contribute.

People should know that they are important to the team not just because a role is filled, but because *they* are filling that role. Maybe someone else could do what they do, but no one could replace who they are. One of the most discouraging things people could believe is that they are not noticed, not known, and not needed; that their contribution doesn't matter, and no one would even realize if they left. When people feel that way for very long, they start making side deals and exit plans, because no one wants to stay where they aren't known and needed.

A leader's job responsibilities include creating a culture that affirms people, involves people, and celebrates people. People aren't anonymous or disposable, and they should never be treated that way. They are visible and valuable, known and needed, accepted and appreciated.

ooo

Recruit through relationship and grow with gratitude, and you'll never lack for loyalty. You'll find the best talent and retain it. You'll build teams that don't just work hard but truly value one another and bring out the best in each other. You'll find yourself leading a team that you love, not because you engaged in some flashy recruitment techniques, but because you know each other and need each other.

KEY TAKEAWAY

If the people on your team and in your organization feel known and needed, they will be motivated to serve together, give their best, and follow your leadership.

What Comes Next?

I hope the subjects we've covered have expanded your thinking and sparked creative ideas for your sphere of leadership. More than anything, though, I hope you are encouraged to continue leading *and* learning: that you invest in refining your leadership, expanding your influence, and honing your people skills for the rest of your life. The goal is not to be obsessed with perfection, but to be obsessed with improvement and a commitment to serve people with excellence.

As you lead *yourself*, you'll grow and evolve into an influential, effective leader. As you lead *others*, you'll bring out the best in them and invite them to join you in your mission. And as you lead *teams*, you'll motivate people to work together to accomplish common goals. The result will be authentic leadership, transformational leadership, servant leadership. It will be a life that is lived not for yourself, but for others; a life that influences and improves and inspires those around you; a life that attempts great things and accomplishes great things.

In the long run, whether you end up with an impressive title, recognition, or even a paycheck, is secondary to the influence you have on others. But it's almost a given that if you serve and lead well, you'll have all that and much more. People need leaders. What comes next is up to you.

Notes

An Invitation to Lead

1. Dr. John C. Maxwell, "Leadership Is Influence: Nothing More, Nothing Less," *Christianity Today*, July 11, 2007,, https://www.christianitytoday.com/pastors/2007/july-online-only/090905.html.

Chapter 1 It Starts with You

1. This quote is often attributed to a speech from John Wesley, but its true source is unknown.

Chapter 2 The Most Important Investment

1. Alex Kennedy (@AlexKennedyNBA), Twitter, March 24, 2018, https://twitter.com/AlexKennedyNBA/status/977629156275048453.

2. Emily Abbate, "The Real-Life Diet of Russell Wilson, Who Plans to Play Football Until He's 45," *GQ*, September 17, 2018, https://www.gq.com/story/russell-wilson-real-life-diet.

3. Adam Wells, "LeBron James' Net Worth: Career Earnings Eclipses $1 Billion," *Bleacher Report*, July 2, 2018, https://bleacherreport.com/articles/2784089-lebron-james-net-worth-career-earnings-eclipses-1-billion.

4. Richard D. Arvey, Maria Rotundo, Wendy Johnson, Zhen Zhang, and Matt McGue, abstract of "The determinants of leadership role occupancy: Genetic and personality factors," *Leadership Quarterly*, vol. 17, issue 1 (February 2006), https://doi.org/10.1016/j.leaqua.2005.10.009.

5. Jan-Emmanuel De Neve, Slava Mikhaylov, Christopher T. Dawes, Nicholas A. Christakis, and James H. Fowler, "Born to lead? A twin design and genetic association study of leadership role occupancy," *Leadership Quarterly*, vol. 24, issue 1 (February 2013), https://doi.org/10.1016/j.leaqua.2012.08.001.

Chapter 3 Find Your Strengths

1. Marcus Buckingham and Donald O. Clifton, *Now, Discover Your Strengths: How to Develop Your Talents and Those of the People You Manage* (New York: The Free Press, 2001), 167.
2. Buckingham and Clifton, *Now, Discover Your Strengths*, 127.
3. Samantha Enslen, "What Does 'in Your Wheelhouse' Mean?" *Quick and Dirty Tips*, September 10, 2019, https://www.quickanddirtytips.com/education/grammar/what-does-in-your-wheelhouse-mean.
4. Buckingham and Clifton, *Now, Discover Your Strengths*, 149.

Chapter 4 Love Yourself, Lead Yourself

1. Roxanne Hai, "Being vulnerable about vulnerability: Q&A with Brené Brown." *TEDBlog*, March 16, 2012, https://blog.ted.com/being-vulnerable-about-vulnerability-qa-with-brene-brown/.
2. Roxanne Hai, "Being vulnerable about vulnerability: Q&A with Brené Brown."
3. Roxanne Hai, "Being vulnerable about vulnerability: Q&A with Brené Brown."

Chapter 5 I Think I Can

1. Bobby Jones, quoted by Zack Pumerantz, "The 100 Best Sports Quotes of All Time," *Bleacher Report*, October 25, 2011, https://bleacherreport.com/articles/910238-the-100-best-sports-quotes-of-all-time#slide13.
2. Andre Agassi, *Open: An Autobiography* (New York: Alfred A. Knopf, 2009), 8–9.
3. Brené Brown, featured on "Brené Brown on the 3 Things You Can Do to Stop a Shame Spiral," *Oprah's Lifeclass*, October 6, 2013, www.Oprah.com/oprahs-lifeclass/Brene-Brown-on-the-3-Things-You-Can-Do-to-Stop-a-Shame-Spiral-Video.
4. Shad Helmstetter, *What to Say When You Talk to Yourself: Powerful New Techniques to Program Your Potential for Success*, Updated Edition (New York: Gallery Books, 1986, 2017), 7–9.
5. Albert Bandura, "Self-Efficacy Mechanism in Human Agency," *American Psychologist* 37, no. 2 (February 1982): 127. https://pdfs.semanticscholar.org/8bee/c556fe7a650120544a99e9e063eb8fcd987b.pdf.
6. Bandura, "Self-Efficacy Mechanism in Human Agency," 123.
7. Bandura, "Self-Efficacy Mechanism in Human Agency," 123.
8. Bandura, "Self-Efficacy Mechanism in Human Agency," 123.

Chapter 6 Awkward Is a Gift

1. Sebastian Thrun, quoted in Lucy Handley, "4 top CEOs reveal what they were like as teenagers—from 'socially challenged' to 'terrible student,'" CNBC, *Make It,*

August 29, 2017, https://www.cnbc.com/2017/08/29/ceos-awkward-teenage-years-and
-how-they-became-successful.html.

2. Sebastian Thrun, featured on "A window into Sebastian Thrun's creative world,"
The Brave Ones, May 10, 2017, https://www.cnbc.com/video/2017/05/10/the-brave
-ones-a-window-into-sebastian-thruns-creative-world.html.

3. Sebastian Thrun, quoted in Lucy Handley, "The education of Sebastian Thrun,"
CNBC, June 1, 2017, https://www.cnbc.com/2017/06/01/sebastian-thrun-udacity-goo
glex.html.

4. Sebastian Thrun, quoted in Lucy Handley, "The education of Sebastian Thrun."

5. Katie A. Lamberson and Kelly L. Wester, "Feelings of Inferiority: A First Attempt to Define the Construct Empirically," *Journal of Individual Psychology* 74, no.
2 (Summer 2018): 172–87.

6. Craig Groeschel (@craiggroeschel), Twitter, March 10, 2018, https://twitter.com
/craiggroeschel/status/972472266243133441?lang=en.

Chapter 7 The Emotionally Healthy Leader

1. Warren Buffett, "Buy American. I Am," *New York Times*, October 16, 2008,
https://www.nytimes.com/2008/10/17/opinion/17buffett.html.

2. Warren Buffett, "Buy American. I Am."

3. Warren Buffett, *Warren Buffett: In His Own Words*, David Andrews, ed. (Evan-
ston, IL: Agate Publishing, 2019), 19.

Chapter 8 Don't Break Your Stride

1. John G. Roberts Jr., "Cardigan's Commencement Address by Chief Justice John
G. Roberts, Jr.," Cardigan Mountain School, June 6, 2017, YouTube video, https://
www.youtube.com/watch?v=Gzu9S5FL-Ug.

2. Thomas Holmes and Richard Rahe, "The Social Readjustment Rating Scale,"
Journal of Psychosomatic Research 11, no. 2 (1967): 213–21, https://doi.org/10.1016
/0022-3999(67)90010-4.

3. Peter G. Northouse, *Leadership: Theory and Practice* (Thousand Oaks, CA:
SAGE Publications, 2019), 224.

4. Stephen Covey, *Principle-Centered Leadership* (Manitou Springs, CO: Summit
Books, 1991), 62.

5. Michael Jordan, quoted in Robert Goldman and Stephen Papson, *Nike Culture:
The Sign of the Swoosh* (New York: SAGE Publications, 1998), 49.

Chapter 9 Becoming Followable

1. Dries Depoorter, "Quick Fix," Dries Depoorter Blog (undated), https://driesde
poorter.be/quickfix/.

2. Simon Kemp, "Digital 2019," *We Are Social*, January 30, 2019, https://wearesoc ial.com/blog/2019/01/digital-2019-global-internet-use-accelerates.

3. Kate Taylor, "Kim Kardashian revealed in a lawsuit that she demands up to half a million dollars for a single Instagram post and other details about how much she charges for endorsements," *Business Insider*, May 9, 2019, https://www.businessinsid er.com/how-much-kim-kardashian-charges-for-instagram-endorsement-deals-2019-5.

4. Anita Hovey, quoted in Chavie Lieber, "The Dirty Business of Buying Instagram Followers," *Vox*, September 11, 2014, https://www.vox.com/2014/9/11/7577585/buy -instagram-followers-bloggers.

5. University of Baltimore, Cheq AI Technologies Ltd., *The Economic Cost of Bad Actors on the Internet: Fake Influencer Marketing in 2019* (Baltimore, MD: University of Baltimore, 2019), https://www.cheq.ai/influencers.

6. Peter G. Northouse, *Leadership: Theory and Practice*, 194.

7. Ralph Waldo Emerson, "The Over-Soul," *Essays: First Series* (Boston: Phillips, Sampson and Company, 1841, 1857), 260.

Chapter 10 Who Are You Listening To?

1. Rob Picheta, "Ethiopian Airlines crash is second disaster involving Boeing 737 MAX 8 in months," *CNN*, March 11, 2019, https://edition.cnn.com/2019/03/10/africa /ethiopian-airlines-crash-boeing-max-8-intl/index.html.

2. Chris Isidore, "These are the mistakes that cost Boeing CEO Dennis Muilenburg his job," CNN Business, December 24, 2019, https://edition.cnn.com/2019/12/24/busi ness/boeing-dennis-muilenburg-mistakes/index.html.

3. "Boeing in Brief," Boeing website, http://www.boeing.com/company/general-info/.

4. Samantha Masunaga, "How the design of Boeing's 737 Max cost CEO Muilen-burg his job," *Los Angeles Times*, December 23, 2019, https://www.latimes.com/busi ness/story/2019-12-23/boeing-737-max-dennis-muilenburg.

5. Aesop, "The Man, the Boy, and the Donkey," Bartleby, March 27, 2001, https:// www.bartleby.com/17/1/62.html.

Chapter 11 Everyone's Favorite Topic

1. Diana I. Tamir and Jason P. Mitchell, "Disclosing information about the self is intrinsically rewarding," *Proceedings of the National Academy of Sciences of the United States of America,* vol. 109, issue 21 (May 2012), 8038–43, https://www.pnas .org/content/109/21/8038.

2. Mor Naaman, Jeffrey Boase, and Chih-Hui Lai, "Is It Really about Me? Message Content in Social Awareness Streams," Rutgers University School of Communication and Information (undated), http://infolab.stanford.edu/~mor/research/naamanCSC W10.pdf.

3. Diana I. Tamir and Jason P. Mitchell, "Disclosing information about the self is intrinsically rewarding."

4. Dick Leonard, *The Great Rivalry: Disraeli and Gladstone* (New York: I.B.Tauris & Co. Ltd, 2013), XX.

5. Karen Huang, Michael Yeomans, A.W. Brooks, J. Minson, and F. Gino, abstract of "It doesn't hurt to ask: Question-asking increases liking," *Journal of Personality and Social Psychology*, vol. 113, no. 3, 430–452 (September 2017), https://doi.org/10 .1037/pspi0000097.

Chapter 12 A Matter of Manners

1. While there's no definitive source, historians often attribute the phrase to William Horman.

2. Gregory Titelman, *The Random House Dictionary of America's Popular Proverbs and Sayings* (New York: Random House, 1996), quoted by BookBrowse. https://www .bookbrowse.com/expressions/detail/index.cfm/expression_number/566/manners -make-the-man-manners-maketh-man.

3. Kevin Clarke, "The papal hand slap divides Catholics and the media," *America*, January 2, 2020, https://www.americamagazine.org/faith/2020/01/02/papal-hand -slap-divides-catholics-and-media.

4. Livia Borghese and Sheena McKenzie, "Pope Francis apologizes for slapping woman's hand on New Year's Eve," *CNN*, January 2, 2020, https://edition.cnn.com /2020/01/01/europe/pope-francis-slap-woman-apology-intl/index.html.

5. William Arthur Ward, *Quotable Quotes: Wit and Wisdom for Every Occasion* (New York: The Readers Digest Association, 1997).

Chapter 13 Reading Rooms, Reading People

1. Leonard Bernstein, *The Joy of Music* (New York: Amadeus Press, 1959, 2004), 160.

Chapter 14 Become Their Biggest Cheerleader

1. William Shakespeare, *Measure by Measure*, Act I, Scene IV, http://shakespeare .mit.edu/measure/full.html.

2. Albert Bandura, "Self-Efficacy," *Encyclopedia of Human Behavior*, vol. 4, V. S. Ramachaudran, ed. (New York: Academic Press, 1994), 71–78, https://web.stanford .edu/~kcarmel/CC_BehavChange_Course/readings/Bandura_Selfefficacy_1994.htm.

3. Albert Bandura, "Self-Efficacy," *Encyclopedia of Human Behavior*.

4. Albert Bandura, "Self-Efficacy," *Encyclopedia of Human Behavior*.

Chapter 15 The Most Important Currency

1. Trista Kelley, "A crypto exchange can't repay $190 million it owes customers because its CEO died with the only password," *Business Insider*, February 4, 2019, https://www.businessinsider.com/quadrigacx-cant-pay-190-million-owed-because-ceo -with-password-died-2019-2.

2. Mohanbir Sawhney and Jeff Zabin, "Managing and Measuring Relational Equity in the Network Economy," *Journal of the Academy of Marketing Science*, vol. 30, no. 4 (2002), 313–332.

3. Mohanbir Sawhney and Jeff Zabin, "Managing and Measuring Relational Equity in the Network Economy."

4. Amos Tversky and Daniel Kahneman, "Advances in prospect theory: Cumulative representation of uncertainty," *Journal of Risk Uncertainty*, vol. 5, 297–323 (1992), https://doi.org/10.1007/BF00122574.

Chapter 16 Narcissism Never Wins

1. "What Are Personality Disorders?" *American Psychiatric Association* (November 2018), physician review by Rachel Robitz, MD, (undated), https://www.psychiatry.org /patients-families/personality-disorders/what-are-personality-disorders.

2. Mayo Clinic Staff, "Narcissistic Personality Disorder," *Mayo Clinic*, (undated), https://www.mayoclinic.org/diseases-conditions/narcissistic-personality-disorder /symptoms-causes/syc-20366662.

3. John Donne, "No Man Is an Island," Meditation XVII, *Devotions upon Emergent Occasions* (1624), public domain.

4. Jean M. Twenge and W. Keith Campbell, *The Narcissism Epidemic: Living in the Age of Entitlement* (New York: Atria Books, 2009), 19.

5. Emily Levine, "A Theory of Everything," *Ted2002* (February 2002), https://www .ted.com/talks/emily_levine_a_theory_of_everything/transcript.

Chapter 17 Time Will Tell

1. Michael Rosenfeld, Reuben J. Thomas, Sonia Hausen, "Disintermediating your friends: How online dating in the United States displaces other ways of meeting," *Proceedings of the National Academy of Sciences*, vol. 116, issue 36 (2019), https:// web.stanford.edu/~mrosenfe/Rosenfeld_et_al_Disintermediating_Friends.pdf.

2. Isabel Thottam, "10 Online Dating Statistics You Should Know," eHarmony, (undated), https://www.eharmony.com/online-dating-statistics/.

3. Janine Willis and Alexander Todorov, "First Impressions: Making Up Your Mind After a 100-Ms Exposure to a Face," *Psychological Science*, vol 17, no. 7 (July 2006), 592–98, https://journals.sagepub.com/doi/10.1111/j.1467-9280.2006.01750.x.

4. "The art of the job hunt," Randstad, October 16, 2018, https://www.randstadusa .com/jobs/career-resources/career-advice/the-art-of-the-job-hunt/631/.

Chapter 18 Listen to Lead

1. Cody Derespina, Chris Ware, Chuck Fadely, Jeffrey Basinger, Matthew Golub, Anthony Carrozzo, Mark La Monica, Robert Cassidy, and Ryan McDonald, "The Evolution of the Pitch," *Newsday*, (undated), https://projects.newsday.com/sports/baseball/pitching-evolution/.

2. "Fastest baseball pitch (male)," *Guinness World Records*, (undated), https://www.guinnessworldrecords.com/world-records/fastest-baseball-pitch-(male)/.

3. Cody Derespina et al., "The Evolution of the Pitch."

4. Phil Rosengren, "7 Tips for Throwing a Better Changeup," *Better Pitching* (2019), https://betterpitching.com/7-tips-for-a-better-changeup/.

5. Karen Huang, Michael Yeomans, Alison Wood Brooks, Julia Minson, and Francesca Gino, "It doesn't hurt to ask: Question-asking increases liking," *Journal of Personality and Social Psychology*, vol. 113, no. 3, (2017), 430–452, https://doi.org/10.1037/pspi0000097.

6. Richard Kraut, "Socrates," *Encyclopedia Britannica* (2020), https://www.britannica.com/biography/Socrates.

7. To list just a few examples: Matthew 15:1–3; Mark 2:1–11; Mark 12:14–24; Luke 10:25–26; John 18:33–34.

Chapter 19 One Conversation Away

1. "2013 Executive Coaching Survey," Stanford GSB Center for Leadership Development and Research, Rock Center for Corporate Governance at Stanford, and The Miles Group (2013), https://www.gsb.stanford.edu/sites/gsb/files/publication-pdf/cgri-survey-2013-executive-coaching.pdf.

2. David F. Larcker, Stephen Miles, Brian Tayan, and Michelle E. Gutman, "2013 Executive Coaching Survey," The Miles Group and Stanford University (August 2013), https://www.gsb.stanford.edu/faculty-research/publications/2013-executive-coaching-survey.

3. Kerry Patterson, Joseph Grenny, Ron McMillan, and Al Switzler, *Crucial Conversations: Tools for Talking When Stakes Are High, Second Edition* (New York: McGraw-Hill Education, 2011), 3.

4. Kerry Patterson et al., *Crucial Conversations*, 9–10.

Chapter 20 Let's Go!

1. Steven D. Greydanus, "An American mythology: Why *Star Wars* still matters," Decent Films (2020), http://decentfilms.com/articles/starwars.

2. Kirell Benzi, "Exploring the *Star Wars* expanded universe (part 1)," Kirell Benzi (2020), https://kirellbenzi.com/blog/exploring-the-star-wars-expanded-universe/.

3. Peter G. Northouse, *Leadership: Theory and Practice* (Thousand Oaks, CA: SAGE Publications, 2015), 5.

4. Northouse, *Leadership*, 372.

5. Gordy Curphy and Dianne Nilsen, "TQ: The Elusive Factor Behind Successful Teams," The Rocket Model, 2020.

6. Gordy Curphy and Dianne Nilsen, "TQ: The Elusive Factor Behind Successful Teams.

7. Brian Houston, @BrianCHouston, Twitter, June 20, 2013, https://twitter.com /brianchouston/status/347838780964741122.

Chapter 21 What Do We Want?

1. Thirty One Bits, "Our story," https://31bits.com/pages/our-story.

2. Esha Chhabra, "How Five College Friends Turned a Social Enterprise Into a Million Dollar Business," *Forbes*, April 1, 2016, https://www.forbes.com/sites/eshach habra/2016/04/01/how-this-social-enterprise-competes-with-instant-gratification-and -rock-bottom-prices/#6e13a3a75e93.

3. "What Is Social Enterprise?" Social Enterprise Alliance (undated), https://social enterprise.us/about/social-enterprise/.

4. Henry D. Thoreau, Letter to H. G. O. Blake, November 16, 1857, quoted in *The Walden Woods Project*, https://www.walden.org/thoreau/mis-quotations/.

5. George Forrest, "The importance of implementing effective metrics," iSixSigma, 2020, https://www.isixsigma.com/implementation/basics/importance-implementing -effective-metrics/.

6. George Forrest, "The importance of implementing effective metrics."

Chapter 22 Chemistry and Culture

1. Alison Beard, "If You Understand How the Brain Works, You Can Reach Anyone," *Harvard Business Review* (March–April 2017), https://hbr.org/2017/03/the-new-science -of-team-chemistry#if-you-understand-how-the-brain-works-you-can-reach-anyone.

2. Suzanne M. Johnson Vickberg, Kim Christfort, "Pioneers, Drivers, Integrators, and Guardians," *Harvard Business Review* (March–April 2017), https://hbr.org/2017 /03/the-new-science-of-team-chemistry#if-you-understand-how-the-brain-works-you -can-reach-anyone.

3. Sam Zell, *Am I Being Too Subtle? Straight Talk from a Business Rebel* (New York: Portfolio, 2017), 181.

4. Sam Zell, *Am I Being Too Subtle? Straight Talk from a Business Rebel*, 181.

5. David Campbell, David Edgar, and George Stonehouse, *Business Strategy: An Introduction,* 3rd ed. (New York: Palgrave, 2011), 263.

Chapter 23 Influencing the Influencers

1. Paul Vallely, "Drug that spans the ages: The history of cocaine," *Independent* (2 March 2006), https://www.independent.co.uk/news/uk/this-britain/drug-that-spans -the-ages-the-history-of-cocaine-6107930.html.

2. Ryan Kucey, "There's a Difference Between Thought Leaders and Influencers," *Better Marketing* (2019), https://medium.com/better-marketing/why-most-influencers -arent-influencing-anyone-62f70567b999.

3. J. Clement, "Number of brand sponsored influencer posts on Instagram from 2016 to 2020," Statista (2020), https://www.statista.com/statistics/693775/instagram -sponsored-influencer-content/.

4. Rachel Hosie, "An Instagram star with 2 million followers couldn't sell 36 T-shirts, and a marketing expert says her case isn't rare," *Business Insider*, May 30, 2019, https://www.businessinsider.com/instagrammer-arii-2-million-followers-cannot-sell -36-t-shirts-2019-5.

5. Denise Brosseau, "What is a thought leader?" Thought Leadership Lab (2020), https://www.thoughtleadershiplab.com/Resources/WhatIsaThoughtLeader.

6. Derek Sivers, "First Follower: Leadership Lessons from a Dancing Guy," sivers .org, February 11, 2010, https://sivers.org/ff.

7. Malcolm Gladwell, *The Tipping Point: How Little Things Can Make a Big Difference* (New York: Back Bay Books, 2002), back cover.

8. Everett M. Rogers, *Diffusion of Innovations*, 5th ed. (New York: Free Press, 2003).

Chapter 24 Is Anyone Listening?

1. Martin Demptster, "Bob MacIntyre confronts partner after his caddie's mum is hit," *The Scotsman*, July 19, 2019, https://www.scotsman.com/sport/golf/bob-macin tyre-confronts-partner-after-his-caddie-s-mum-is-hit-1-4968277.

2. *Golf Rules Illustrated: The Official Illustrated Guide to the Rules of Golf, 2012– 2015.* (London: Hamlyn, 2012).

3. See, for example, "Why Do Golfers Shout 'Fore!'?" Leading Britain's Conversation, Global (2020) https://www.lbc.co.uk/radio/special-shows/the-mystery-hour/sport -games/why-do-golfers-shout-fore-114876/.

4. Quoted by Nicholas Fearn, *The Latest Answers to the Oldest Questions: A Philosophical Adventure with the World's Greatest Thinkers* (New York: Grove Press, 2007), 93.

5. Andy Stanley, *Communicating for a Change: Seven Keys to Irresistible Communication* (Colorado Springs, CO: Multnomah, 2006), 104.

Chapter 25 Meetings Matter

1. Patrick Lencioni, *Death by Meeting: A Leadership Fable about Solving the Most Painful Problem in Business* (San Francisco, CA: Jossey-Bass, 2004), viii.

2. Elise Keith, "55 Million: A Fresh Look at the Number, Effectiveness, and Cost of Meetings in the U.S.," Lucid Meetings, December 4, 2015, https://blog.lucidmeetings .com/blog/fresh-look-number-effectiveness-cost-meetings-in-us.

3. Michael Mankins, "This Weekly Meeting Took Up 300,000 Hours a Year," *Harvard Business Review*, April 29, 2014, https://hbr.org/2014/04/how-a-weekly-meeting-took -up-300000-hours-a-year.

4. Patrick Lencioni, *Death by Meeting*, viii.

5. Patrick Lencioni, *Death by Meeting*, 235.

6. Roy. F. Baumeister, "The Psychology of Irrationality: Why People Make Foolish, Self-Defeating Choices," Isabelle Brocas and Juan D. Carrillo, eds., *The Psychology of Economic Decision-Making, Vol. 1: Rationality and Well-Being* (Oxford: Oxford University Press, January 2003), 12–13.

7. Richard L. Brandt, "Birth of a Salesman," *Wall Street Journal*, October 15, 2011, https://www.wsj.com/articles/SB10001424052970203914304576627102996831200.

Chapter 26 Work Your Systems

1. John Holusha, "W. Edwards Deming, Expert on Business Management, Dies at 93," *New York Times*, December 21, 1993, https://www.nytimes.com/1993/12/21/obituaries /w-edwards-deming-expert-on-business-management-dies-at-93.html.

2. Andrea Gabor, "He Made America Think About Quality," *Fortune*, October 30, 2000, https://archive.fortune.com/magazines/fortune/fortune_archive/2000/10/30 /290646/index.htm.

3. Andrea Gabor, "Quality Revival, Part 2: Ford Embraces Six Sigma," *New York Times*, June 13, 2001, https://andreagabor.com/selected-articles/management-quality -revival-part-2-ford-embraces-six-sigma/.

4. Andrea Gabor, "Quality Revival, Part 2."

5. John Deming, "W. Edwards Deming Quotes," *The W. Edwards Deming Institute*, 2020, https://quotes.deming.org/.

6. "PDSA Cycle," *The W. Edwards Deming Institute* (2020), https://deming.org/ex plore/p-d-s-a.

7. IHI Multimedia Team, "Like Magic? ('Every system is perfectly designed . . .')," Institute for Healthcare Improvement, August 21, 2015, http://www.ihi.org/communi ties/blogs/_layouts/15/ihi/community/blog/itemview.aspx?List=7d1126ec-8f63-4a3b -9926-c44ea3036813&ID=159.

8. John Deming, "W. Edwards Deming Quotes," *The W. Edwards Deming Institute* (2020), https://quotes.deming.org/.

9. Craig Bloem, "Why Successful People Wear the Same Thing Every Day," *Inc.*, February 20, 2018, https://www.inc.com/craig-bloem/this-1-unusual-habit-helped -make-mark-zuckerberg-steve-jobs-dr-dre-successful.html.

Chapter 27 Known and Needed

1. Andy Staples, "A History of Recruiting: How Coaches Have Stayed a Step Ahead," *Sports Illustrated*, June 23, 2008, https://www.si.com/more-sports/2008/06/23/recruiting-main.

2. Kyle Bonagura, "Too Young for Division I?" *ESPN*, October 23, 2017, http://www.espn.com/espn/feature/story/_/id/20924695/10-year-old-maxwell-bunchie-young-touted-next-big-thing-football-coaches-bought-in.

3. Pat Forde, "With Milestone Recruiting Class, Clemson's Dominance Reaches New Heights," *Sports Illustrated*, December 18, 2019, https://www.si.com/college/2019/12/18/clemson-football-recruiting-dabo-swinney.

4. Jim Collins, *Good to Great: Why Some Companies Make the Leap . . . and Others Don't* (New York: Harper Business, 2011), 54.

5. Jim Collins, *Good to Great*, 13.

Chad Veach is an author, an international speaker, and lead pastor of Zoe Church in Los Angeles, California. His heart for pouring into the next generation led Chad to serve as a youth pastor for fifteen years and as the director of a college internship program for organizational management before establishing Zoe in 2014. Chad is the host of *Leadership Lean In*, a discussion-based podcast about cultivating leadership, influence, creativity, and relationships. He and his wife, Julia, reside in the Los Angeles area with their four children: Georgia, Winston, Maverick, and Clive. Learn more at www.zoechurch.org.